Geological Society of America
Memoir 173

Glacial Lake Wisconsin

Lee Clayton and John W. Attig
Wisconsin Geological and Natural History Survey
3817 Mineral Point Road
Madison, Wisconsin 53705

1989

Published by The Geological Society of America, Inc.
3300 Penrose Place, P.O. Box 9140, Boulder, Colorado 80301

GSA Books Science Editor Campbell Craddock

Printed in U.S.A.

Library of Congress Cataloging-in-Publication Data

Clayton, Lee.
    Glacial Lake Wisconsin / Lee Clayton and John W. Attig.
        p.   cm. — (Memoir ; 173)
    Includes bibliographical references.
    ISBN 0-8137-1173-8
        1. Paleolimnology—Wisconsin—Wisconsin, Lake (Glacial lake)
    2. Glacial epoch—Wisconsin—Wisconsin, Lake (Glacial lake)
    3. Wisconsin, Lake (Wis. : Glacial lake)   I. Attig, John W.
    II. Title.   III. Series: Memoir (Geological Society of America) ;
    173.
    QE39.5.P3C53   1989
    551.7′92′09775—dc20   89-27582
                                                                                          CIP

10 9 8 7 6 5 4 3 2

Contents

Abstract 1

Introduction 3

Setting 4

The Basins of Lake Wisconsin 5

Outlets 7
   Northwestern outlets 7
      Morrison and McKenna saddles 8
      East Fork Black River 8
      South Bluff outlet 8
      North Bluff outlet 8
      West Babcock outlet 11
      North Babcock outlet 11
      Factors determining outlet used 11
      Earlier northwestern outlets 13
   Dells outlet 14
   Alloa outlet 14
   Outlets of southern basins 14
      Mirror Lake outlet 14
      Lower Narrows outlet 15
      Man Mound saddle 15
      Baraboo outlet 15
      Upper Narrows outlet 16
      Narrows Creek outlet 16
      Loganville/Reedsburg saddle 16
      Excelsior saddle 17
      Hogback outlet 18
   Devils Lake outlet 19
   Sauk City and Badger outlets 21

Shorelines 21
   Preservation 21
   Evidence of shorelines 22
      Outlets 22
      Shore terraces 22
      Ice-rafted erratics 23
      Offshore deposits 23

Shore-ice collapse trenches 23
Shore cliffs and stacks 24
Shoreline-profile model 24
Shoreline profiles 27
Wyeville shoreline 29
Elderon shoreline 31
Pre-Wyeville shorelines 33
Precision 34
Accuracy 34

Offshore Sediment 34
Offshore silt in main basin 36
Offshore sand in main basin 36
East of the Wisconsin River 36
West of the Wisconsin River 37
The Lewiston sand trap 39
Offshore sediment in other basins 39

Final Drainage 39
The Alloa flood 40
The Dells flood 42
The flood down the Wisconsin River 44

Permafrost 44

Chronology 46

Great Lakes Crustal Rebound 48

Conclusion 48

Acknowledgment 48

A Photo Essay of Glacial Lake Wisconsin Area 49

References 79

Geological Society of America
Memoir 173
1989

Glacial Lake Wisconsin

ABSTRACT

During the last part of the Wisconsin Glaciation, central Wisconsin was occupied by a proglacial lake called Lake Wisconsin. Lake Wisconsin formed when the Green Bay Lobe of the Laurentide Ice Sheet reached the Baraboo Hills in south-central Wisconsin, damming the lowland to the north, which is now occupied by the south-flowing Wisconsin River. At its greatest extent the lake was 115 km long, and its greatest depth was 50 m.

Lake Wisconsin occupied a number of separate but interconnected topographic basins, including a main basin and seven smaller basins to the south of the main basin. During most of its history, Lake Wisconsin drained to the northwest through one of several outlets, all of which emptied into the Black River, a tributary of the Mississippi River. Sometime before the maximum expansion of the Green Bay Lobe during the Wisconsin Glaciation, Lake Wisconsin emptied southward through the Devils Lake outlet to the Wisconsin River, a tributary of the Mississippi River. At the end of Lake Wisconsin's existence, it drained to the southeast out the Alloa outlet, to the Wisconsin River. The southern basins drained, at various times, through various combinations of a dozen separate outlets.

Wind, slope wash, soil creep, cryoturbation, and solifluction have destroyed most of the beach ridges and terraces of Lake Wisconsin. Based on elevations of the few remaining beaches plus the elevations of the lake outlets, ice-rafted erratics, offshore deposits, the break in slope at the west edge of the outwash plain on the east side of the main basin, and shore-ice collapse trenches, we have been able to reconstruct three shorelines; from oldest to youngest, these are: the Wyeville shoreline, which has been tilted S45°W at 0.1 m/km; the Johnstown shoreline, tilted S60°W at 0.6 m/km; and the Elderon shoreline, tilted S55°W at 0.3 m/km. They intersect each other along a northwest-southeast line through the northwestern outlet. The shorelines are tilted because the Earth's crust had been depressed under the weight of the glacier but later rebounded with the removal of the weight.

The Wyeville shoreline probably formed about 19,000 years ago when Lake Wisconsin first came into existence as the glacier expanded into central Wisconsin during the last part of the Wisconsin Glaciation. The Johnstown shoreline formed about 15,000 years ago when the glacier was at its maximum extent and the Earth's crust was at its maximum depression. The Elderon shoreline formed about 14,000 years ago, just before the lake finally drained, after the crust had begun to rebound as the glacier wasted back near the end of the Wisconsin Glaciation.

Tens of meters of offshore sand was deposited in the deep basins of glacial Lake Wisconsin. Much of this sand is included in the Big Flats Formation. The sand was deposited in part by density currents derived from glacial meltwater rivers. In most areas, one or more beds of offshore silt occur within the sand sequence; the uppermost one (the New Rome Member) was probably deposited somewhat before the Johnstown Phase of glaciation.

The final drainage of Lake Wisconsin was probably catastrophic. As the Green Bay Lobe wasted from the east end of the Baraboo Hills, the narrow ice dam was breached by water from the lake, causing the water level in the Lewiston basin to drop tens of meters, probably within a few days. This caused water from the main basin and other southern basins to flood into the Lewiston basin through a breach in the Johnstown moraine; this flood at least partly cut the sandstone gorges at the Wisconsin Dells.

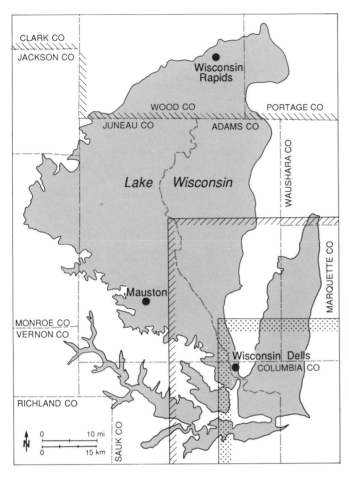

Figure 1. Map of central Wisconsin showing areas of Pleistocene geologic maps in the area of Lake Wisconsin (shaded). The location of the lake within Wisconsin is shown in Figures 2 and 3. The hatched area to the north is that mapped by Weidman (1907) and that to the southeast is the area mapped by Alden (1918). Reports by Clayton (1986, 1987, 1989a, 1989b) and Clayton and Attig (in preparation) contain geologic maps of Portage, Adams, Wood, Juneau, and Sauk Counties. The dotted area in the southeast was mapped by Socha (1984).

INTRODUCTION

Between about 19,000 and 14,000 years ago, during the last part of the Wisconsin Glaciation, central Wisconsin was occupied by a proglacial lake called Lake Wisconsin. At its greatest extent, Lake Wisconsin was about 115 km long, roughly the size of modern Great Salt Lake in Utah, and it was as deep as 50 m. The existence of Lake Wisconsin has been known for more than a century, and many of its large-scale features have been known for the past 70 years. However, even though the lake occupies an important position in the Pleistocene history of the region, it has received little detailed attention until recently, and no comprehensive report on the lake is available.

The purpose of this memoir is to report recent findings and to relate these to our modern understanding of the late Pleistocene history of the western Great Lakes region. After a brief discussion of the geologic setting, the basic geometric framework of the lake is described, and a working set of names is applied to the various lake basins and outlets. The middle section of the memoir is an evaluation of the evidence for three of the highest shorelines and a description of the offshore sediment. This is followed by speculation on the catastrophic floods that may have occurred when the lake finally drained. The last sections deal with the relationships between the lake and the history of perma-

frost of the area, the evidence for the chronology of various lake events, and the relationship between tilting of the Earth's crust during glaciation in the Lake Wisconsin area and in the Great Lakes area.

The person who discovered Lake Wisconsin is unknown, but the earliest geologists to recognize the moraine across the Baraboo Hills probably realized that the glacier must have dammed a lake in the Wisconsin River valley to the north. Scattered observations on the lake occur in the geological literature of the late nineteenth and early twentieth centuries. Salisbury and Atwood (1900, p. 129–132), for example, gave some evidence for the lake. Nevertheless, Weidman (1907), who mapped the geology of central Wisconsin including the northern part of the Lake Wisconsin plain (Fig. 1), made no mention of the lake; he thought the sand as far south as Necedah was deposited by interglacial rivers (Plate 2, p. 518–520, 546).

Alden (1918) was the first to thoroughly document the existence of Lake Wisconsin. His report covered the Pleistocene geology of southeastern Wisconsin, which included the southeastern part of the lake plain (Fig. 1). The part of the lake in the Baraboo valley was referred to both as Baraboo Lake and as Lake Baraboo, and the rest was referred to as Lake Wisconsin. He

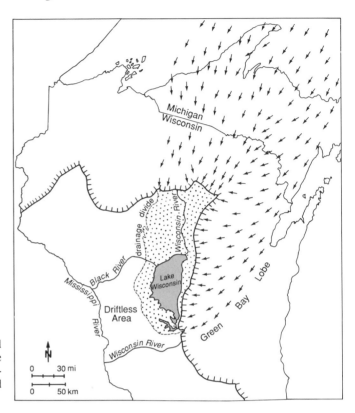

Figure 2. Map of Wisconsin showing location of Lake Wisconsin and the maximum extent of the ice during the Wisconsin Glaciation (line with tick marks). Dots indicate the drainage basin that supplied non-meltwater sediment to the lake. Arrows indicate ice-flow direction and area supplying meltwater sediment to the lake.

documented a number of occurrences of beach and offshore sediment and located the various basins and many of their outlets. Topographic maps at a scale of 1:62,500 had recently become available for southeastern parts of the lake basin, and as a result, shoreline elevations could be reported with considerable confidence. Martin (1916) cited a preliminary copy of Alden's report and reproduced many of his findings in his *Physical Geography of Wisconsin* (nearly identical editions were published in 1932 and 1965). He outlined the history of the lake and its main features as they were to be known for the next several decades.

During the 1930s, the Civilian Conservation Corps and the Forest Protection Division of the Wisconsin Conservation Department drilled 7-m exploration wells at about 0.8-km intervals throughout much of the main basin of Lake Wisconsin (unpublished logs in files of Wisconsin Geological and Natural History Survey). Information on the distribution of offshore silt and clay in the well logs was summarized by Harloff (1942).

Recent studies of the lake have benefited from improved topographic maps. No topographic maps were available in much of the northern and central part of the area until the 1950s; at that time 1:250,000 maps with 100-ft and 50-ft contour intervals were prepared by the Army Map Service. During the 1970s and 1980s, 1:24,000 topographic maps with 20-ft, 10-ft, or 5-ft contour intervals first became available in much of the northern part of the area, and they are now available for the entire area. Partly as a result of the availability of these high-quality topographic maps, the Wisconsin Geological and Natural History Survey in 1982

began mapping the Pleistocene geology of Portage, Adams, Wood, Juneau, and Sauk Counties (published scale 1:100,000; Clayton, 1986, 1987, 1989a, 1989b; Clayton and Attig, in preparation; Brownell, 1986). These counties include most of the area of Lake Wisconsin, with the main exception of the southeastern basin (Fig. 1), the southern half of which has been mapped by Socha (1984). The present report is based in large part on information collected as a result of this county-mapping program.

Locations in this memoir are given in two different ways. General locations of features having considerable areal distribution are described in terms of the public land survey (section, township, and range). Points are more precisely located using Universal Transverse Mercator (UTM) coordinates.

SETTING

Wisconsin is south of Lake Superior and west of Lake Michigan. During the last part of the Wisconsin Glaciation, lobes of the Laurentide Ice Sheet flowed southwest out of Ontario, through the lake basins, to central Wisconsin. Lake Wisconsin was dammed on the east by the Green Bay Lobe of the ice sheet (Fig. 2). On the south, the lake was bounded by the Baraboo Hills. To the west of the lake, a divide separated the drainage west to the Mississippi River from drainage east to the Lake Michigan basin and the St. Lawrence River. On the north, the lake was bounded by the highlands of northern Wisconsin.

Earlier versions of Lake Wisconsin may have existed before

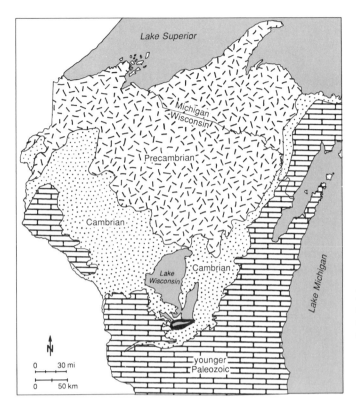

Figure 3. Map of Wisconsin showing bedrock geology and the location of Lake Wisconsin. The black area in southern Wisconsin is the outcrop area of the Baraboo quartzite. The Precambrian rock of northern Wisconsin and Michigan includes a variety of igneous and metamorphic rock. The Cambrian rock is largely sand and sandstone. The younger Paleozoic rock is largely dolomite and limestone, with some sandstone and shale. A comparison with Figure 2 will suggest the different kinds of material supplied to Lake Wisconsin.

the last part of the Wisconsin Glaciation, but little evidence is available for this. During the last part of the Wisconsin Glaciation, Lake Wisconsin came into existence when the Green Bay Lobe reached the Baraboo Hills, perhaps around 19,000 years ago. The lake may have drained and refilled during glacial fluctuations, but for a few thousand years, during the maximum expansion of the glacier, the lake probably remained fairly stable, with water discharging from its northwest outlet. The ice margin then began to retreat, and the lake drained when the ice wasted from the east end of the Baraboo Hills, roughly 14,000 years ago. The lake may have refilled and drained during glacial fluctuations at this time.

The position and shape of the basins of Lake Wisconsin are related to the distribution of pre-Pleistocene rock types (Fig. 3). Precambrian igneous and metamorphic rock of the Canadian Shield crops out in the northern part of the state and in the central part along the Wisconsin Arch. This generally hard rock is resistant to erosion, and the land slopes gently southward and to the east and west off the arch.

Late Cambrian sandstone occurs in a band 10 to 100 km wide through the middle of the state. Much of this sandstone, in the Mt. Simon Formation, is poorly lithified and underlies lowlands such as the one in central Wisconsin that was occupied by Lake Wisconsin.

Younger Paleozoic dolomite, limestone, and sandstone form abrupt north-facing escarpments across southern Wisconsin. The stratigraphically lowest and northernmost of these is the Wo-

newoc escarpment, formed by resistant sandstone of the Cambrian Wonewoc Formation. The Wonewoc escarpment, which rises tens of meters above the southwestern margin of the main basin of Lake Wisconsin, encloses several of the smaller southern basins of the lake.

The Precambrian Baraboo quartzite projects up through the sandstone at the south end of the Lake Wisconsin plain (Fig. 3). This extremely hard, resistant quartzite forms the Baraboo Hills (Fig. 4). Lake Wisconsin came into existence when the Green Bay Lobe moved onto the steep, abrupt east end of the Baraboo Hills.

THE BASINS OF LAKE WISCONSIN

Lake Wisconsin occupied a number of separate basins (Fig. 4), which are described in this section. Although at different times these basins were interconnected in different ways, most often the connections were by narrow straits. The bodies of water in these basins could have been given separate names, but this would require a complex of names that would change every time the lake level and the interconnections changed. Instead, names are here attached to the separate basins, which retained fairly stable configurations through the period being discussed.

The name Lake Wisconsin is here used for all combinations of bodies of water in the various basins that were at nearly the same level at any one time and were the result of the glacial dam at the east end of the Baraboo Hills. For this reason, the name

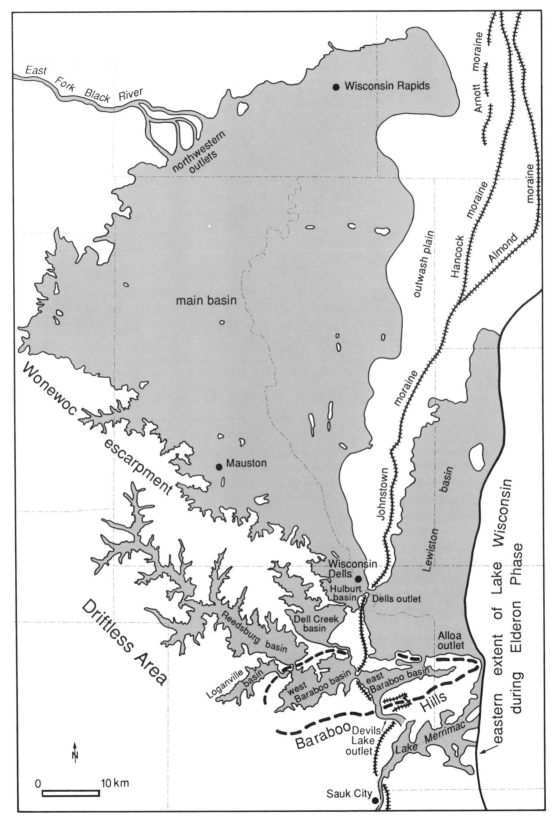

Figure 4. Map of central Wisconsin showing the main features of Lake Wisconsin. The map shows the approximate maximum extent of the lake during the last part of the Wisconsin Glaciation; it never occupied this entire area at any one time. The heavy dashed line is the crest of the Baraboo Hills.

Lake Baraboo, which has been attached to the bodies of water in the Reedsburg, Loganville, and east and west Baraboo basins (Fig. 4), is not used as long as the water was at nearly the same level as the water in the Lewiston and Dell Creek basins, but it is retained for a body of water at higher elevations.

The name Lake Wisconsin is also used for the reservoir that has existed since 1914 above the dam across the Wisconsin River at Prairie du Sac, in the Lake Merrimac area (Fig. 4). Although the glacial lake was named before the reservoir, the reservoir is locally much better known. No confusion should result here, however, because this memoir contains no other reference to present-day Lake Wisconsin.

The term main basin is used here for the Lake Wisconsin basin north of the Wonewoc escarpment and west of the outwash plain beyond the outer moraine of the Green Bay Lobe (Fig. 4). During most of the last part of the Wisconsin Glaciation, the southern end of the main basin was connected to a small basin, here called the Hulburt basin, through a broad strait. Upstream from the Hulburt basin is a basin here called the Dell Creek basin. The two basins that are separated by the Johnstown moraine at the city of Baraboo are here referred to as the east and west Baraboo basins. Like the main basin, the Hulburt, Dell Creek, and west Baraboo basins are confined on their eastern sides by the outwash plain of the Green Bay Lobe. The Baraboo basins are bounded on the south by the South Range and on the north by the North Range of the Baraboo Hills. Upstream from the west Baraboo basin are the Loganville and Reedsburg basins. The Hulburt, Dell Creek, Reedsburg, and Loganville basins occupy valleys extending back into the Wonewoc escarpment. Lewiston basin is the name used here for the basin that was bounded on the west by the Johnstown moraine and on the east by the ice of the Green Bay Lobe. The east Baraboo basin and the Lewiston basin are separated by the North Range of the Baraboo Hills.

Sometime before the Johnstown moraine and outwash plain formed, the east and west Baraboo basins were one continuous basin. This basin was connected by a broad strait to the Dell Creek basin, which was connected to the Lewiston and main basins to form one large basin.

Modern Devils Lake occupies a basin in Devils Lake gorge, which was probably an outlet of Lake Wisconsin sometime before the Johnstown moraine formed (Fig. 4). After the Devils Lake outlet was dammed by glacial material but before the Johnstown moraine formed, the Devils Lake basin probably held an arm of Lake Wisconsin. When the ice stood at the Johnstown moraine, Devils Lake was an independent proglacial lake, about 40 m above Lake Wisconsin, into which it drained. Just before Lake Wisconsin drained for the last time, the body of water in the Devils Lake basin might have been part of Lake Wisconsin, connected to the body of water in the east Baraboo basin by a narrow channel.

South of Lake Wisconsin, and contemporaneous with the part of it in the Lewiston basin, was a completely separate proglacial lake, Lake Merrimac, dammed behind the Johnstown moraine (Fig. 4). Its surface was about 30 m lower than that of Lake

Wisconsin. The ice dam at the east end of the Baraboo Hills separated Lake Wisconsin from Lake Merrimac.

OUTLETS

More than a dozen separate outlets carried water out of Lake Wisconsin or from one basin to another at various times (Fig. 4). Each outlet is briefly described. The outlets played an important role in the history of the lake because they determined the water level in the lake; today they are major pieces of evidence for the location of the shorelines.

Northwestern outlets

The main outlet from Lake Wisconsin through most of its history was to the northwest down the Black River to the Mississippi River (Figs. 2 and 4). Whenever the two southern outlets from Lake Wisconsin (the Devils Lake outlet and the Alloa outlet) were blocked, water had to discharge here across the next lowest point on the drainage divide surrounding the lake. The exact location of this outlet (or outlets) is obscure, however, because the lowest saddles on the divide between the Black and Wisconsin River valleys are broad, flat areas of swamp and sand dunes without obvious channels. The channels that must once have existed here have been largely obliterated by later lacustrine, fluvial, and eolian activity.

The northwest edge of the lake plain in the main basin is not well marked. The flat, sandy lake plain grades westward above the highest probable lake level with no noticeable break, and the plain continues west across the drainage divide in several places (for example, at Morrison saddle, described in the next section) and down into the flat sand plain of the Black River valley in Jackson County (Fig. 5). This sand plain has been interpreted to have been cut by fluvial or slope processes (Clayton and Madison, 1983); it was thought not to be a lake plain, because no way was known that a lake could have been dammed there during the Wisconsin Glaciation.

However, the Jackson plain may have been covered by a lake long before the Wisconsin Glaciation, and water may have flowed in the reverse direction, from the Black River valley to the Wisconsin River valley. Knox and Attig (1988), as well as earlier workers, have recognized an eastward glacial advance ending several kilometers east of the mouth of the Wisconsin River (Fig. 2), probably in Middle or Early Pleistocene time; the glacier blocked the Wisconsin valley and caused the Wisconsin River to flow eastward. A glacier there, or anywhere else between the mouths of the Wisconsin and Black Rivers, would dam a lake in the upper Mississippi valley, including the Black River valley. This or another lake in the Black River valley could have been contemporaneous with and connected to the one farther west in the Chippewa River valley in which the Kinnickinnic silt was deposited; this lake was dammed by the glacier that deposited the Hersey till in the lower part of the Chippewa valley (Baker, 1984, p. 7, Fig. 2). The outlet of lakes such as these would have been

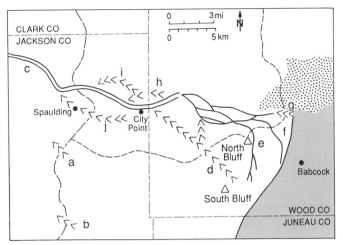

Figure 5. Map of northwestern outlets of Lake Wisconsin. a: Morrison saddle. b: McKenna saddle. c: East Fork Black River. d: South Bluff outlet. e: North Bluff outlet. f: west Babcock outlet. g: north Babcock outlet. h: Hay Creek outlet. i: Davidson Creek outlet. j: Spaulding outlet. The approximate position of Lake Wisconsin during the Johnstown Phase of glaciation is shown with gray tone. The fan of the Yellow River and Hemlock Creek is shown with a dotted pattern. Possible outlets lacking a visible channel form are shown with nested arrow heads. Outlets that retain an obscure channel form are single lines. A conspicuous channel form is indicated by a double line. The long-dash line is the preglacial drainage divide, and the short-dash line is the modern drainage divide between the Black River valley and the Wisconsin River valley. The county boundaries in relation to the rest of Lake Wisconsin are shown in Figure 1.

east across the low point of the divide between the Black and Wisconsin valleys, at the subsequent location of the northwest outlet of Lake Wisconsin (Fig. 5).

Morrison and McKenna saddles. Alden (1918, p. 223) thought the northwestern outlet of Lake Wisconsin was in east-central Jackson County, where low, peat-filled saddles occur at the drainage divide east of the headwaters of Morrison and McKenna Creeks, which are tributary to the Black River (Fig. 5a and b). In 1974, Black (p. 149–150) noted that topographic maps were still inadequate to alter this conclusion.

Martin (1916, p. 321) recognized, however, that these saddles are too high to have been outlets during the Wisconsin Glaciation. Topographic maps available today show that the Morrison saddle (Fig. 6) is about 2 km wide at an elevation of about 307 m, and the McKenna saddle is about 1 km wide at an elevation of about 306 m. These saddles are about 10 m higher than the lowest saddles across the divide in Wood County (Fig. 5), and the difference in elevation would have been even greater before crustal tilting occurred after the ice sheet melted.

It is possible, however, that the Morrison or McKenna saddles or higher saddles to the southwest were outlets of an earlier version of Lake Wisconsin, prior to the Wisconsin Glaciation. Attig and Muldoon (1989) and Clayton (1989a) give evidence that a glacier advanced southeastward to the northwest edge of Lake Wisconsin at least once (during the Milan Phase of glaciation), and possibly more than once, in middle or early Pleistocene time or possibly late Pliocene time. If this advance coincided with an advance of the Green Bay Lobe that dammed an earlier version of Lake Wisconsin, the more northern outlets may have been blocked by ice, causing the Morrison or McKenna saddles to be used.

East Fork Black River. Martin (1916) recognized that the East Fork Black River (Fig. 5c) carried the water from Lake Wisconsin during the Wisconsin Glaciation. West of Wood

County, this outlet retains a channel form (Fig. 7). There, the channel is about 0.5 km wide, with cutbanks several meters high. Its banks were cut in Cambrian sandstone, and it is bottomed on Precambrian igneous and metamorphic rock. In Wood County, the channel has been at least in part filled with peat and fluvial and eolian sand deposited after Lake Wisconsin drained. As a result it here retains at most only an obscure channel form.

Martin, however, did not locate the exact position of the outlet across the divide between the Wisconsin and Black River valleys. The next several paragraphs discuss possible divide crossings. None of these retains a clear channel form like the East Fork Black River in Jackson County because the outlets were cut in easily eroded Pleistocene sand rather than in sandstone or were later buried by postlacustrine sediment.

South Bluff outlet. Modern topographic maps show that the lowest point on the divide between the Wisconsin and Black River valleys is in a broad, flat area of swamp and sand dunes 4 to 6 km wide between South Bluff, North Bluff, and Kurt Creek, around Sec.11,T.21N.,R.2E. (Fig. 5d). The swamp throughout this area is between the 970-ft and 975-ft (296-m and 297-m) contours (Fig. 8). This hypothetical outlet is here referred to as the South Bluff outlet.

No channel can be seen through the area today, however, perhaps because it was never used as an outlet. More likely, the channel form has been destroyed by eolian erosion, or the channel has been filled with later fluvial, eolian, and swamp sediment. Drill holes indicate more than 7 m of sand, peat, and clay in some parts of this area (Harloff, 1942).

North Bluff outlet. A more conspicuous outlet is here called the North Bluff outlet (Fig. 5e). It crosses the divide between the Wisconsin and Black River valleys 0.5 km northeast of North Bluff, in Sec.5,T.21N.,R.3E. The lowest point on the divide here is between the 975-ft and the 980-ft (297-m and 299-m) contours (Fig. 9). This outlet is marked by a channel-like sag

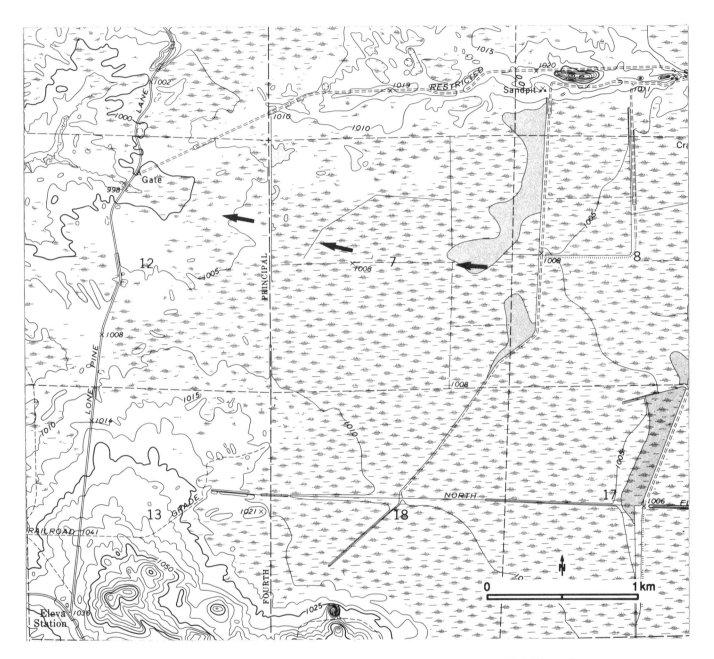

Figure 6. Topographic map of the Morrison saddle. The drainage divide between the Black River valley (west) and the Wisconsin River valley (east) crosses the area from south-southwest to north-northeast through section 7; water from Lake Wisconsin would have flowed westward through section 7, as shown by the arrows, if the lake were ever this high (307 m or 1,008 ft). U.S. Geological Survey Spaulding Quadrangle (7.5 minute series; 5-ft contour interval; 1970). The location (T.21N.,R.1W. and R.1E.) is shown in Figure 5.

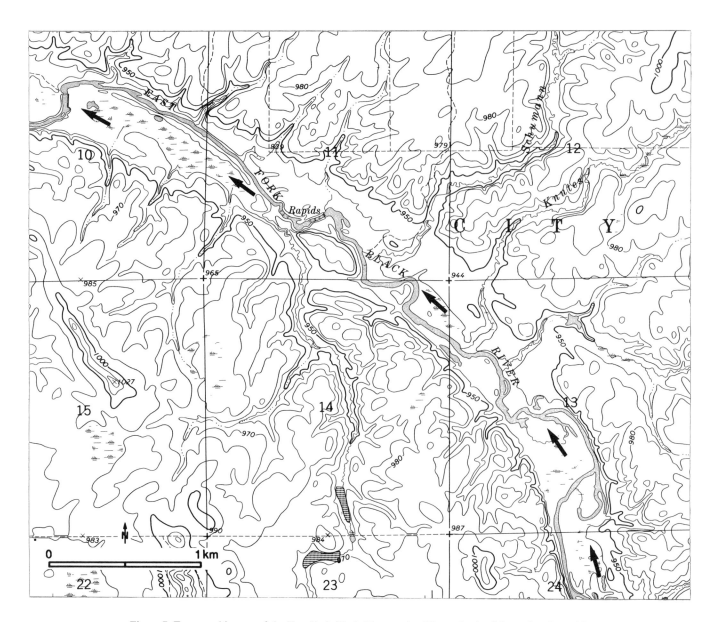

Figure 7. Topographic map of the East Fork Black River outlet. The cutbank of the outlet channel is near the 950-ft contour. Flow is indicated by the arrows. U.S. Geological Survey City Point NW Quadrangle (7.5 minute series; 10-ft contour interval; 1970). The location (T.22N.,R.1W.) is shown in Figure 5.

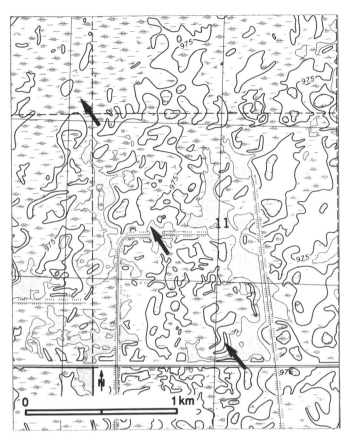

Figure 8. Topographic map of the general area of the hypothetical South Bluff outlet. No channel has been identified here, but water probably flowed from Lake Wisconsin northwestward through this area, as suggested by the arrows. The drainage divide between the Black River valley and the Wisconsin River valley is indefinite, but it crosses somewhere through the area shown here from southwest to northeast. All of the small hills shown here are eolian dunes. U.S. Geological Survey's Quail Point Flowage Quadrangle (7.5 minute series; 5-ft contour interval; 1984). The location (T.21N.,R.2E.) is shown in Figure 5.

now only 1 or 2 m deep through the swamp and sand dunes in Sec. 35 and 36,T.22N.,R.2E., Sec.31,T.22N.,R.3E., and Sec. 5, 8, and 17,T.21N.,R.3E.

A test hole augered in the middle of the sag at point **a** in Figure 9 showed 2 m of peat over 20 m of sand over silt and clay (Fig. 10). An east-west ground-penetrating-radar profile through this point shows a buried depression more than 8 m deep and about 0.5 km wide in the same position as the surface sag. The radar image shows that it is filled with cross-bedded sand. A test hole near the side of the sag at point **b** in Figure 9 showed 2 m of peat over 4 m of sand over Cambrian sandstone. A test hole near the middle of the sag 1.2 km west-northwest of **b** in Figure 9 showed 3 m of peat over 10 m of sand over Cambrian sandstone. This information indicates that the North Bluff channel was probably at least 8 m deep when it functioned as an outlet of Lake Wisconsin.

West Babcock outlet. Another possible outlet, here called the west Babcock outlet, occurs at **f** in Figure 5. This obscure sag through the swamp and sand dunes occurs 2 km west of Babcock, 3 km east of the North Bluff channel.

An east-west ground-penetrating-radar profile through point **c** in Figure 9 shows a buried scarp at the west edge of the sag, with 2 m of sand on sandstone west of the sag and more than 9 m of Pleistocene fill in the sag. Drill holes here (Harloff, 1942) showed that sandstone occurs on the west side of the sag, and 1 m

of peat, 4 m of sand (fluvial, lacustrine, or eolian), and 2 m of clay (lacustrine?) occur under the sag. Where this sag crosses the divide between the Wisconsin and Black River valleys at **d** in Figure 9, the low point is now between the 980-ft and 985-ft (299-m and 300-m) contours but was probably below the 980-ft contour before the sand dunes were deposited here. A drill hole here (Harloff, 1942) indicated more than 7 m of sand.

North Babcock outlet. Another hypothetical outlet, here called the north Babcock outlet (g in Fig. 5), is at a low point in the divide 5 km north-northwest of Babcock, to the northeast of the west Babcock outlet. The elevation here is between 980 and 985 ft (299 and 300 m). No channel form is present, perhaps because it has been buried by the Yellow River fan since the lake drained (shown in Fig. 5). Drill holes here (Harloff, 1942) indicated more than 7 m of sand.

Factors determining outlet used. Each of these four proposed northwestern outlets—the South Bluff, North Bluff, west Babcock, and north Babcock—may have actually been an outlet of Lake Wisconsin. The factors influencing which outlet was used at any one time are discussed in the following paragraphs.

The degree to which the Earth's crust had been tilted by the weight of the glacier probably helped determine which outlet was used. At the beginning of a period during which Lake Wisconsin was dammed by the glacier, when the Earth's crust was tilted the least steeply to the northeast, the more southwesterly of these

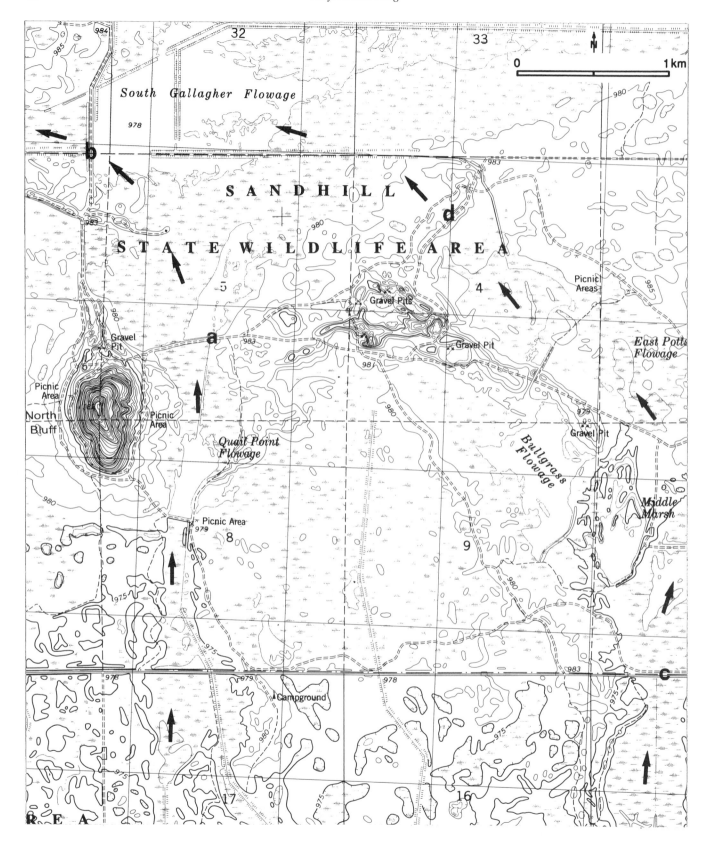

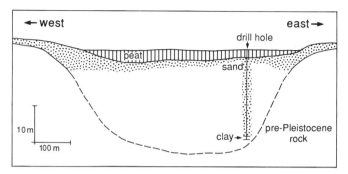

Figure 10. East-west cross section through North Bluff outlet through point **a** on Figure 9. Vertical line indicates drill hole; rest of section is based on a ground-penetrating-radar profile.

outlets were more likely to have been used. During the height of a glaciation, when the crust was tilted the most steeply to the northeast, the more northeasterly of these outlets were more likely to have been used. Near the end of a lacustrine period, when the crust was again less steeply tilted, the outlet might have shifted back to the southwest.

In addition, the fan of Yellow River, shown in the upper right part of Figure 5, probably had an influence on which outlet was used. At the surface, this fan consists of fluvial sand deposited after the lake drained. Its thickness and internal makeup are unknown, but it seems likely that a fluvial fan was active before the lake came into existence and also during any low-water periods between the major lake stages. In addition, offshore sediment was probably deposited on the fan when the lake existed. The growth of the fan would prevent the more northeasterly outlets from being used. During the height of glaciation, outlets to the northeast of the north Babcock outlet (Fig. 5g) might have been used—if so, they have been completely buried by the Yellow River fan and no evidence of them is now known.

The North Bluff and the Babcock outlets are now nearly filled with sediment that was probably in large part deposited by the Yellow River when it occupied the southwest corner of its fan after the lake drained. The orientation of channel scars on the upper part of the fan indicates that the Yellow River sometimes flowed west to the East Fork Black River. At the present time it flows south, just east of the west Babcock channel (1 km east of the east edge of the area shown in Fig. 9). At other times it probably flowed south through the North Bluff and west Babcock channels, which are now occupied by south-flowing tributaries of the Yellow River (the reverse of the direction of the lake outlet).

An additional factor affecting outlet use is the thickness of easily eroded Pleistocene and Cambrian sediment and the depth to resistant Precambrian rock. Near the present drainage divide, the material under most of the outlets initially was Pleistocene sediment overlying thin Cambrian sandstone on Precambrian rock. Test drilling has shown that the outlets are still bottomed on sandstone in some places near the divide, but west of City Point (Fig. 5) the channel is largely bottomed on Precambrian rock. The outlet rivers probably quickly cut down to a Precambrian sill somewhere along the reach near the divide, which would cause them to stabilize at that elevation. However, the outlets would also tend to shift back and forth as the Earth's crust tilted back and forth due to glacial loading and unloading, and the outlets would gradually downcut as lower paths across the Precambrian-rock surface were encountered. Precambrian rock occurs at a depth of more than 23 m below the present surface of the North Bluff outlet at point **a** in Figure 9, but it is at the land surface within a few hundred meters of either side of the channel, which probably tended to stabilize the outlet in that position.

Earlier northwestern outlets. Possible predecessors of the East Fork Black River outlet include the Hay Creek outlet (Fig. 5h): the saddle across the local drainage divide there is now between the 965-ft and 970-ft (294-m and 296-m) contours, a few meters above the East Fork Black River outlet. A possible earlier Davidson Creek outlet passed through a saddle now between the 970-ft and 980-ft (296-m and 299-m) contours (Fig. 5i). A possible still earlier outlet, the Spaulding outlet, occurs east of Spaulding where the saddle is now between the 980-ft and the 985-ft (299-m and 300-m) contours (Fig. 5j). The elevation of the water surface or of the channel bottom in these outlets is

Figure 9. Topographic map of the North Bluff (**a, b**) and west Babcock (**c, d**) outlets (indicated by arrows). Points **a, b, c,** and **d** are locations of drill holes and radar profiles discussed in the text. The drainage divide between the Black River valley and the Wisconsin River valley crosses northeast-southwest through North Bluff. North Bluff and some of the hills in section 4 are composed of Precambrian rock, but most of the other low hills in this area are eolian dunes. U.S. Geological Survey's Quail Point Flowage Quadrangle (7.5 minute series; 5-ft contour interval; 1984). The location (T.21 and 22 N.,R.3E.) is shown in Figure 5.

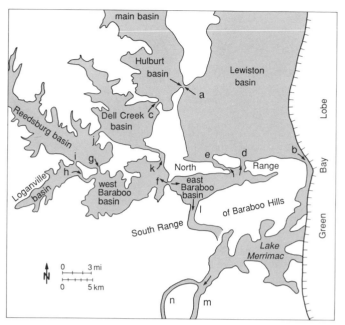

Figure 11. Map showing the various outlets in the southern part of Lake Wisconsin. The margin of the ice during the Elderon Phase of the Wisconsin Glaciation is indicated by a line with tick marks. a: Dells outlet. b: Alloa outlet. c: Mirror Lake outlet. d: Lower Narrows outlet. e: Man Mound saddle. f: Baraboo outlet. g: Upper Narrows outlet. h: Narrows Creek outlet. i: Loganville/Reedsburg saddle. j: Excelsior saddle. k: Hogback outlet. l: Devils Lake outlet (through the South Range of the Baraboo Hills). m: Sauk City outlet. n: Badger outlet. Arrows indicate direction of flow.

obscure because the amount of post-outlet erosion and the amount of recent fill is unknown.

Dells outlet

During the height of the Wisconsin Glaciation, the Green Bay Lobe stood at the Johnstown moraine (Fig. 4), and the Lewiston basin was filled with glacial ice rather than water, but after the glacier wasted a short distance back from the moraine, water began to fill the Lewiston basin. By the time the glacier had wasted back a few kilometers, meltwater from at least 200 km to the north was flowing into the north end of the Lewiston basin. This water left the basin through a breach in the moraine at its low point, which will here be referred to as the Dells outlet (Figs. 4 and 11a).

Water from the Lewiston basin drained westward through the Dells outlet until the Alloa outlet (Figs. 4 and 11b) opened, which caused the water level in the Lewiston basin to suddenly drop and the flow in the Dells outlet to reverse; water flowed from the Hulburt and main basins eastward through the Dells outlet to the Lewiston basin. This flood probably quickly deepened the Dells outlet and cut the sandstone gorges that in this area are referred to as dells. The Wisconsin Dells are discussed in more detail in a later section on the final draining of the lake.

Alloa outlet

Alloa outlet is the name used here for the outlet at the southeast corner of the Lewiston basin (Fig. 4). This outlet func-

tioned whenever the glacier margin was at lake level at the east end of the Baraboo Hills (Fig. 11b).

The last time the Alloa outlet was used was when the Green Bay Lobe had wasted back from the Johnstown moraine to near the position of one of the youngest Elderon moraines (Fig. 4). Water began to flow through the Alloa outlet when the lake level was about 295 m. More information on the Alloa outlet is given in a later section on the final draining of the lake.

Two probable successors of the Alloa outlet occur just to the east of it. One, in the north half of Sec.30,T.12N.,R.9E., is a saddle at an elevation of about 245 m; the other, in the southwest part of Sec.29,T.12N.,R.9E., is a saddle at an elevation of about 238 m.

Outlets of southern basins

Mirror Lake outlet. The Mirror Lake outlet, at the Mirror Lake overpass of Interstate Highway 90-94 (UTM coordinates BD736-288), carried water from the Dell Creek basin to the Hulbert basin (Fig. 11c; Fig. 12). Today the outlet is a sandstone gorge about 100 m wide and 35 m deep. In preglacial time, Dell Creek flowed southeastward, about 5 km south of the Mirror Lake outlet. When water drained from the main basin of Lake Wisconsin through its northwest outlet, the Mirror Lake gorge was about 0.5 km long and perhaps several meters deep, but after drainage shifted to the Alloa outlet, water drained catastrophically from the Dell Creek basin, and the Mirror Lake outlet was probably cut to below the present level of Mirror Lake, forming a sandstone gorge 5 km long.

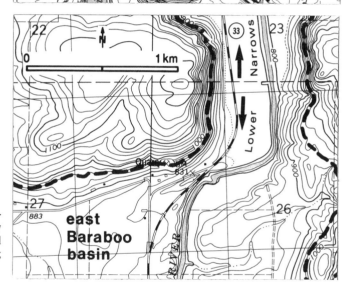

Figure 12. Topographic map of the Mirror Lake outlet (arrow indicates flow direction). The heavy dashed line is the shoreline during the Elderon Phase of glaciation (the topographic bench at the same elevation is not a shore terrace but is caused by the resistant Ironton Member at the top of the Wonewoc Formation). The divided highway is Interstate 90 and 94. U.S. Geological Survey Wisconsin Dells South Quadrangle (7.5 minute series; 10-ft contour interval; 1975). The location (Sec.29, T.13N.,R.6E., on the south side of the village of Lake Delton) is shown in Figure 11.

Figure 13. Topographic map of the Lower Narrows outlet (arrows indicate that water flowed north or south at different times). The heavy dashed line is the shoreline during the Elderon Phase. U.S. Geological Survey Baraboo Quadrangle (7.5 minute series; 20-ft contour interval; 1975). The location (T.12N.,R.7E.) is shown in Figure 11.

Lower Narrows outlet. The Lower Narrows outlet carried water from the east Baraboo basin to the Lewiston basin (Fig. 4; Fig. 11d). The Lower Narrows today is a gorge about 0.5 km wide and 1 km long through the Precambrian quartzite of the North Range of the Baraboo Hills. The floor of the gorge today is occupied by the Baraboo River and is about 55 m below the level of Lake Wisconsin when it flowed out the northwest outlet (Fig. 13). Like the Devils Lake outlet through the South Range of the Baraboo Hills (discussed in later paragraphs), the Lower Narrows was probably cut by a preglacial river rather than by discharging lake water.

Man Mound saddle. A possible predecessor of the Lower Narrows outlet (when it was still covered by glacial ice) occurs 3 km to the west in the NW¼ of Sec.28,T.12N.,R.7E., 0.5 km northwest of Man Mound Park (Fig. 11e). The modern saddle here is between the 940-ft and 960-ft (287-m and 293-m) contours, near the level of Lake Wisconsin when it flowed out the northwest outlet. No channel form is obvious there today.

Baraboo outlet. The Baraboo outlet carried water from the east Baraboo basin to the west Baraboo basin between the time the Green Bay Lobe melted back from the Johnstown moraine and the time the Lower Narrows outlet opened (Fig. 4; Fig. 11f). However, it had to carry water in the reverse direction, from the west Baraboo basin to the east Baraboo basin, while the Lower Narrows outlet was in use because the Lower Narrows and Baraboo outlets were much lower than any other possible outlet from the west Baraboo basin. The Baraboo outlet is just west of the community of West Baraboo, in the SW¼ Sec.34,T.12N.,R.6E.

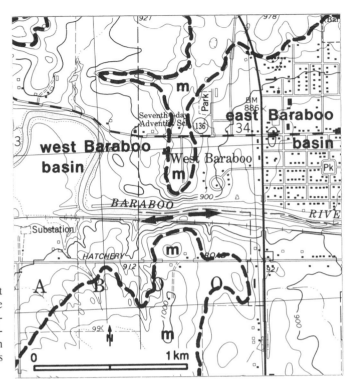

Figure 14. Topographic map of the Baraboo outlet (arrows indicate that water flowed east or west at different times). The heavy dashed line is the shoreline during the Elderon Phase. **m:** Johnstown moraine. The north-south highway is U.S. 12. U.S. Geological Survey North Freedom Quadrangle (7.5 minute series; 20-ft contour interval; 1975). The location (T.12N.,R.6E., at the southwest edge of village of West Baraboo) is shown in Figure 11.

(Fig. 14). It is a gorge about 0.2 km wide and 0.3 km long and is occupied by the Baraboo River, which today is about 25 to 30 m below the level of Lake Wisconsin when it flowed out the northwest outlet. It was cut through the Johnstown moraine, down to Precambrian quartzite.

Upper Narrows outlet. The Upper Narrows outlet carried water from the Reedsburg basin to the west Baraboo basin (Fig. 4; Fig. 11g). If the Excelsior outlet ever functioned (Fig. 11j; discussed in a later paragraph), the Upper Narrows may also have carried water in the reverse direction, from the west Baraboo basin to the Reedsburg basin. The Upper Narrows, which has also been called the Rock Springs Gorge and Ablemans Gorge, is about 0.2 km wide and 1 km long. The present bottom of the gorge, which is occupied by the Baraboo River, is 10 to 30 m below the level of Lake Wisconsin when it flowed out a northwest outlet (Fig. 15). The gorge has been cut through the Precambrian quartzite of the North Range of the Baraboo Hills, probably—like the Devils Lake outlet (discussed in later paragraphs)—well before it became a lake outlet.

Narrows Creek outlet. The Narrows Creek outlet carried water from the Loganville basin to the west Baraboo basin (Fig. 4; Fig. 11h). Like the Upper Narrows outlet, the gorge was probably cut in preglacial time through Baraboo quartzite. It is about 0.2 km wide and 1 km long. Its present bottom, which is occupied by Narrows Creek, in the NW¼ Sec.31,T.12N.,R.5E., was about 5 to 25 m below the level of Lake Wisconsin when it flowed out the northwest outlet.

Loganville/Reedsburg saddle. A possible drainageway between the Loganville and Reedsburg basins (Fig. 4; Fig. 11i) exists in the middle of Sec.24,T.12N.,R.4E., 4 km west-northwest of the Upper Narrows. Modern topographic maps show a saddle here between the 940-ft and 960-ft (287-m and 293-m) contours (Fig. 16).

No outlet existed here during the maximum of the Wisconsin Glaciation, when the northwest outlet was depressed relative to this saddle, causing the saddle to be well above the level of Lake Wisconsin. However, the northwest outlet was less depressed when Lake Wisconsin first came into existence and just before it drained (see later discussion of shoreline profiles). Therefore, the water level may have been as high as the saddle at these two times, but no evidence is known that the water actually flowed through this saddle. It seems more likely that the major flow from the Loganville and Reedsburg basins was always out the much deeper Narrows Creek and Upper Narrows outlets.

Excelsior saddle. The lowest saddle between the Reedsburg and Dell Creek basins is in Excelsior township, in the NW¼ Sec. 9 and SW¼ Sec.4,T.12N.,R.5E., 7 km east of Reedsburg (Fig. 4; Fig. 11j). Modern topographic maps show the saddle to be between the 960-ft and 980-ft (293-m and 299-m) contours (Fig. 17).

Alden (1918, p. 222) mentioned this as a possible outlet, and a map by Martin (1916, Fig. 132) shows a strait at this point. As will be shown in the later discussion of shoreline profiles, the saddle was between about 13 and 20 m above the level of Lake

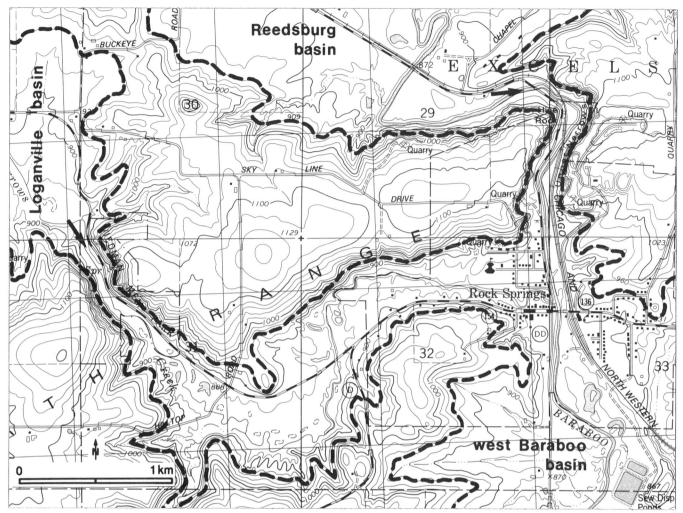

Figure 15. Topographic map of the Upper Narrows and Narrows Creek outlets (flow directions indicated by arrows). The heavy dashed line is the shoreline during the Elderon Phase. U.S. Geological Survey Rock Springs Quadrangle (7.5 minute series; 20-ft contour interval; 1975). The location (T.12N.,R.5E.) is shown in Figure 11.

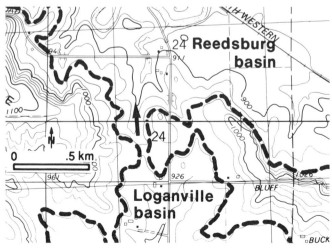

Figure 16. Topographic map of the Loganville/Reedsburg saddle (arrow indicates possible flow of water from the Loganville basin to the Reedsburg basin). The heavy dashed line is the shoreline during the Elderon Phase. The area shown in the southeast corner of Figure 16 overlaps the area shown in the northwest corner of Figure 15. U.S. Geological Survey Rock Springs and Reedsburg East Quadrangles (7.5 minute series; 20-ft contour interval; 1975). The location (T.12N.,R.4E.) is shown in Figure 11.

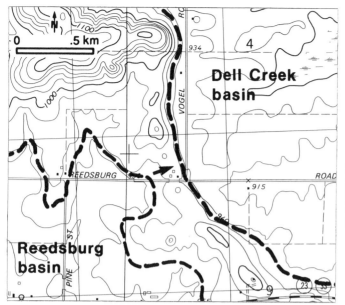

Figure 17. Topographic map of the Excelsior saddle (arrow indicates possible flow from the Reedsburg basin to the Dell Creek basin). The heavy dashed line is the shoreline during the Elderon Phase. U.S. Geological Survey Reedsburg East Quadrangle (7.5 minute series; 20-ft contour interval; 1975). The location (T.12N.,R.5E.) is shown in Figure 11.

Wisconsin when the Green Bay Lobe stood at the Johnstown moraine, and it was between about 2 and 11 m above the water level just before the lake finally drained. If the water had risen high enough in the Reedsburg basin to spill across this saddle, a channel would have been cut through the soft sandstone of the narrow ridge here; however, there is no evidence of a channel. It is unlikely that the Excelsior outlet actually ever existed, at least not during the last part of the Wisconsin Glaciation.

Hogback outlet. When the glacier stood at the Johnstown moraine, water had to find some route from the Reedsburg, Loganville, and west Baraboo basins to the Dell Creek basin (Fig. 4). The lowest saddle is 5 km northwest of the city of Baraboo, on the north side of Hogback Ridge, in the S½ Sec.17,T.12N.,R.6E.; this hypothetical outlet is here referred to as the Hogback outlet (Fig. 11k). Modern topographic maps show the low point on the divide to be between the 960-ft and 970-ft (293-m and 296-m) contours (Fig. 18).

Alden (1918, p. 222) suggested this as a possible outlet, but Martin (1916, Fig. 132) showed no outlet here. As will be shown in the later discussion of shoreline profiles, the saddle was between about 9 m and 14 m above the level of Lake Wisconsin when it stood at the Johnstown moraine, and it was between about 1 and 6 m above the water level just before the lake finally drained. The Hogback outlet is more likely than the Excelsior outlet to have carried water because it was at least a few meters lower. However, as at the Excelsior saddle, there is no obvious

channel. Nevertheless, water had to drain somewhere from the Reedsburg, Loganville, and west Baraboo basins when the glacier was at the Johnstown moraine. Because this was the lowest point in the divide to the north of the basins, an outlet must have existed here. The Hogback outlet was probably forced up against the base of Hogback Ridge by the growth of the outwash plain originating from the glacier 3 km to the east. If so, it cut into the soft sandstone here and oversteepened the north slope of Hogback Ridge. As a result it seems probable that the outlet was later buried under fans of stream sediment and hillslope debris eroded off the ridge after the outlet ceased functioning, as well as by outwash.

The precise elevation of this hypothetical buried outlet is unknown, so it is unclear if the water level in the west Baraboo, Loganville, and Reedsburg basins was much above the water level in the Dell Creek, Hulburt, and main basins. Before the outwash plain was built west of the Johnstown moraine, the Hogback outlet (and any earlier outlet just to the east) should have flowed freely, and the water in the west Baraboo basin should have been nearly at the same elevation as the water in the rest of Lake Wisconsin. The outlet probably maintained a low gradient as the outwash forced it up against the sandstone of Hogback Ridge, but if any well-cemented sandstone debris from the hillside restricted the outlet, the gradient might have increased, causing Lake Baraboo to be several meters above Lake Wisconsin.

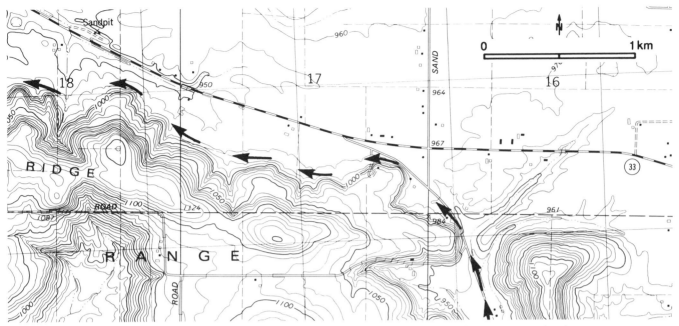

Figure 18. Topographic map of the area of the Hogback outlet. The arrows indicate the suggested path of the outlet channel, which is now buried under outwash and by material washed down from Hogback Ridge. The flat area is the outwash plain west of the Johnstown moraine. U.S. Geological Survey Wisconsin Dells South Quadrangle (7.5 minute series; 10-ft contour interval; 1975). The location (T.12N.,R.6E.) is shown in Figure 11.

Devils Lake outlet

Devils Lake and its gorge are the center of attraction in Devils Lake State Park, a unit of the Ice Age National Scientific Reserve (Fig. 19), which has been described by Attig and others (1989c). The Devils Lake outlet had to have carried water out the south end of early versions of Lake Wisconsin, before the gorge was clogged by the Johnstown or older moraines (Fig. 4; Fig. 11). The present Devils Lake gorge is 1 km wide, 5 km long, and 140 m deep. Along the sides of the gorge are talus cones derived from cliffs of Baraboo quartzite. The present elevation of Devils Lake is 294 m, and its bottom is at 280 m (Alden, 1918, p. 41). The crest of the Johnstown moraine where it crosses the gorge east and north of the lake is at an elevation of about 320 m. Water from proglacial Devils Lake cut a channel through the north moraine, perhaps down to below the level of modern Devils Lake, but probably not down to the level of Lake Wisconsin (about 283 m); if the channel was cut deeper than at present, it was later refilled to just above the level of modern Devils Lake with sediment deposited by the small stream now entering the northeast corner of Devils Lake.

Devils Lake gorge was at least 100 m deeper before the Pleistocene fill was deposited. The deepest known well (Wisconsin Geological and Natural History Survey Geologic Log Sk-17) in the gorge shows Pleistocene sediment below an elevation of 184 m.

The gorge was first cut in Late Cambrian time or earlier. Late Cambrian sandstone is present in the gorge near lake level at the southwest corner of Devils Lake (Dalziel and Dott, 1970, Plate 1), indicating that the gorge through the quartzite was cut at least to that level before the sandstone was deposited. Paleozoic rock occurs high on the flanks of the Baraboo Hills, indicating that the gorge was completely buried during Paleozoic time. The gorge, as we see it today, was exhumed sometime after the fluvial gravel of the Windrow Formation was deposited at the top of the East Bluff of the gorge in Cretaceous or Cenozoic time (Thwaites and Twenhofel, 1921, p. 296).

Chamberlin (1883, p. 284–285), Alden (1918, p. 105–107), and others thought the gorge either was originally cut by the preglacial Wisconsin River or was later exhumed by it. They thought the Wisconsin River flowed through the gorge until it was blocked by the Johnstown moraine in late Pleistocene time. However, we know of no reason to think that the preglacial Wisconsin River ever did flow through the gorge.

The present Wisconsin River consists of four segments with independent histories. Segment 1, from Lac Vieux Desert to Merrill in northern Wisconsin, formed at the end of the Wisconsin Glaciation and is unrelated to the preglacial drainage. Segment 2 is the reach that flowed south in preglacial time from Merrill to Stevens Point (this is the segment shown north of Lake Wisconsin and south of the glacier in Fig. 2). From Stevens Point, preglacial segment 2 flowed southeast through southern Portage County

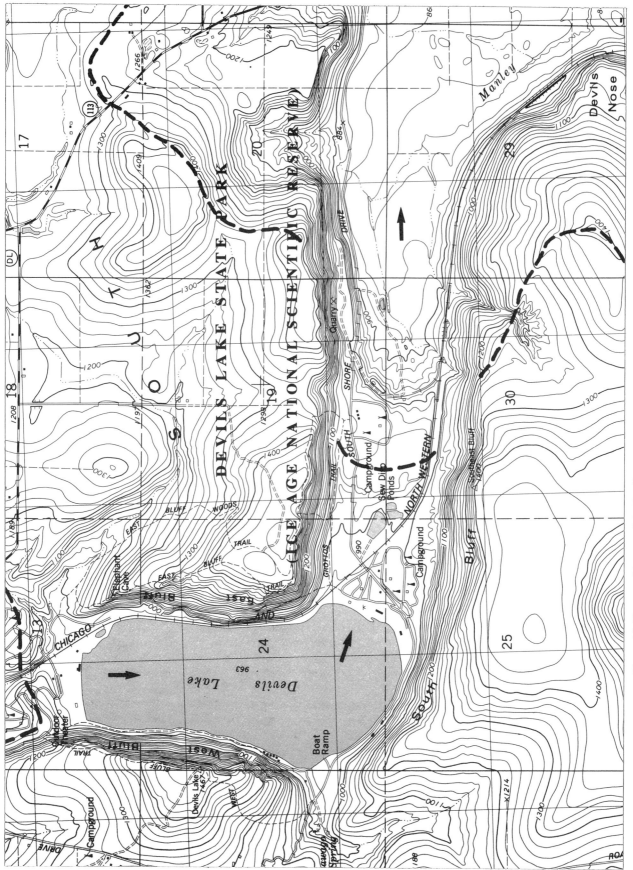

Figure 19. Topographic map of the Devils Lake gorge. The arrows indicate flow of water from Lake Wisconsin sometime before the Johnstown moraine was formed. The crest of the Johnstown moraine is indicated by a heavy dashed line. U.S. Geological Survey Baraboo Quadrangle (7.5 minute; 20-ft contour interval; 1975). The location (T.11N.,R.6 and 7E.) is shown in Figure 11.

(county boundaries are shown in Fig. 1), but beyond that, its course is unclear because the form of the sub-Pleistocene surface is too poorly known (Clayton, 1986). Segment 3 was established in Pleistocene time when the Green Bay Lobe funneled the water from the northern segment into Lake Wisconsin; this path was maintained after the lake drained because the thick glacial deposits east of the lake prevented it from escaping that way. This segment runs across thick lake sediment and is unrelated to the preglacial drainage in central Wisconsin. Segment 4 is an east-west reach between Lake Wisconsin and the Mississippi River (Fig. 2). It might have been connected to a preglacial Marquette River northeast of the Baraboo Hills (Stewart, 1976, p. 34–83). The name Wisconsin River might reasonably be attached to the preglacial versions of either segment 2 or 4.

Where might preglacial segment 2 have flowed southeast of Stevens Point? The preglacial valleys of the Lemonweir and Yellow Rivers drained the areas west and northwest of Lake Wisconsin (Fig. 2) and sloped southeastward through the southeastern corner of Adams County (Clayton, 1987, Fig. 6). It seems likely that preglacial segment 2 would have been intercepted by the Lemonweir-Yellow valley, and their combined flow probably continued into the lowlands to the southeast of Adams County. We know of no reason to think that preglacial segment 2 ever flowed anywhere near the Baraboo Hills. Similarly, the surface of the Cambrian rock along the path of segment 4 east of the Baraboo Hills is at an elevation of 135 m (Knox and Attig, 1988, p. 568), apparently well below the bottom of the quartzite gorge at Devils Lake, indicating that the preglacial Wisconsin defined by segment 4 more likely went that way. If the gorge was exhumed by a through-flowing preglacial river, it was probably not the Wisconsin River or any river with a similar course.

Another possible explanation for the present gorge is that local preglacial streams, aided by slope processes, partly exhumed the gorge by removing Paleozoic sandstone down to below the elevation of the future outlet of Lake Wisconsin. This might have involved a single through-flowing stream, but it could have involved two small streams flowing in opposite directions from a saddle. This is known to have been an effective process because streams no longer than a few kilometers have been able to flush the Cambrian sandstone from numerous other quartzite gorges on the flanks of the Baraboo Hills; an example is Pine Creek, southwest of Baraboo.

Further exhumation could have been carried out by a river flowing out of Lake Wisconsin. If a proglacial lake ever existed in the Black River valley (as suggested in the discussion of the northwest outlets) at a time the Green Bay Lobe covered the east end of the Baraboo Hills, water from that lake emptied into Lake Wisconsin, and water from the two lakes would have had to discharge through the Devils Lake gorge.

If, however, water from the lake in the Black River valley had never flowed this way, the first glacier to reach the east end of the Baraboo Hills would have dammed an early version of Lake Wisconsin. The lake would have risen to the level of the Devils Lake saddle, providing it was then below the level of the north-

west outlet—that is, below roughly the elevation of modern Devils Lake. Water would then have spilled from the lake, flowing across the saddle and flushing sandstone out of the gorge.

Such a river would have been highly erosive. It would probably have had a drainage basin larger than any preglacial Wisconsin River, and because it would also have been carrying meltwater from a few hundred kilometers of glacier margin, it would probably have had greater discharge than any preglacial Wisconsin River. As a result, any outlet river from Lake Wisconsin could have rapidly downcut through the easily eroded sandstone.

Once the quartzite gorge was exhumed (to at least 100 m below modern Devils Lake), only a small Lake Wisconsin could have existed, in the extreme southeastern part of the basin. A full-sized Lake Wisconsin could have existed again only when the ice blocked the gorge at Devils Nose (lower right-hand corner of Fig. 19), forcing the lake to again discharge to the northwest. The Devils Lake outlet had to continue to operate any time the ice was between Devils Nose and the eastern end of the Baraboo Hills. But once the gorge was clogged above lake level by a moraine, the northwest outlet, rather than the Devils Lake outlet, operated when the ice covered the east end of the Hills.

A moraine formed in the gorge during the last part of the Wisconsin Glaciation, but the gorge might have been first clogged by a moraine during an earlier glaciation. In central Wisconsin, the Arnott moraine (Fig. 4) was formed beyond the Johnstown moraine sometime before the last part of the Wisconsin Glaciation, probably before the first part as well (Clayton, 1986), and an equivalent moraine might have formed at the Devils Lake outlet.

Sauk City and Badger outlets

Two final outlets that should be mentioned are the Sauk City and Badger outlets (Fig. 4; Fig. 11m and n). Although they were never outlets of Lake Wisconsin but were the outlets of Lake Merrimac, they are involved in later discussions of the drainage of Lake Wisconsin. Lake Merrimac came into existence when the Green Bay Lobe wasted back from the Johnstown moraine. Its first outlet—the Badger outlet—was 6 km north of Sauk City, in Sec.23 and 24, T.10N.,R.6E. It is 0.3 km wide and about 10 m deep. When Lake Wisconsin finally drained, the outlet of Lake Merrimac shifted to the Sauk City area. The resulting channel is 0.5 km wide and 30 m deep.

SHORELINES

Preservation

The general location of Lake Wisconsin has long been known, but the approximate location of its upper shorelines has been known only in the southern part of the lake (Alden, 1918; Martin, 1916). The shoreline position is poorly known because shore features are poorly preserved. No beach ridge or terrace can be recognized along most of the uppermost shorelines, which formed between about 19,000 and 15,000 BP, and in the few places where a ridge or terrace has been recognized, preservation is poor. In comparison, the upper beaches of proglacial Lake Superior, which formed around 9,500 BP, are well preserved and can be traced nearly continuously (Clayton, 1984); the beaches of Lake Michigan that formed around 11,000 BP are similarly well preserved (Goldthwait, 1907; Thwaites and Bertrand, 1957). Lake Wisconsin had a similar fetch and so should have originally had beaches of similar size. Greater age, in itself, is not an adequate explanation for the much poorer preservation.

Wind erosion may be a partial explanation. Most of the Pleistocene sediment in the area of Lake Wisconsin consists almost entirely of sand and therefore is easily eroded by the wind. The Lake Wisconsin beaches were probably also mostly sand, but the few beach deposits that are preserved are primarily in areas where there is a gravel source, such as around the quartzite bluff at Necedah in the middle of the main basin. In contrast, most beaches of proglacial Lake Superior contain gravel and therefore are resistant to wind erosion.

The Lake Wisconsin beaches are probably also poorly preserved because of erosional processes related to permafrost. No permafrost is known to have existed during or after the formation of the Lake Superior and Lake Michigan beaches, but there is a great deal of evidence for continuous permafrost on the plain of Lake Wisconsin after it drained, until about 13,000 BP (this evidence is discussed in a later section of this memoir).

When the sand is unfrozen, most rain infiltrates, but when permafrost is present, much more soil erosion is possible because most of the rain runs off. In addition, enhanced soil creep, cryoturbation, and solifluction all probably tended to destroy the beaches when permafrost was present.

Whatever the cause, shore features of Lake Wisconsin are poorly preserved and therefore must be analyzed carefully and at considerable length. The following sections of this report are devoted to an evaluation of the scattered evidence for the position of the shorelines at various times.

Evidence of shorelines

One of the main goals of this study has been to reconstruct the position of Lake Wisconsin's shorelines. If a shoreline were known to be horizontal, a single firmly documented observation of a beach would be adequate to precisely establish the position of the shore throughout the lake basin. However, there is no evidence that the shorelines of Lake Wisconsin are horizontal. Instead, tilting of the Earth's crust due to the weight of the glacier is to be expected. For this reason, all available evidence on shoreline position has to be considered, including the elevation of lake outlets, shore terraces, shore deposits, ice-rafted erratics, offshore deposits, a break in slope on the outwash plain at the east edge of the main basin, channel scars, shore-ice collapse trenches, and shore stacks. Each of these kinds of information will be briefly evaluated in the following paragraphs, and they are plotted on shore profiles that will then be discussed.

Outlets. The water level in a lake is controlled by the elevation of the outlet and by the depth of water in the outlet. For most of its life, Lake Wisconsin's outlet was to the northwest, so we are concerned here primarily with the elevation of the northwest outlets, which have been described in a previous section. A lake outlet generally has two points whose elevations can be accurately measured: the bottom of the channel and the top of channel cutbanks. The elevations of the bottoms of the northwest outlets are poorly known because they have been filled with later sediment. However, outlets as wide as these would be expected to be several meters deep, and the lake level should have been somewhat above the elevation of the channel bottom. We therefore have assumed that most shoreline features were formed when discharge through the outlet was near the bank-full stage, and we have generally drawn the shoreline just below the top of the bank on the shoreline profiles. These elevations have been interpolated from topographic maps with a 5-ft (1.5-m) contour interval. Water levels based on these outlet elevations are judged to be within several meters of the true values.

Shore terraces. Probable shore terraces have been recognized in several places. A typical shore terrace consists of a wave-cut terrace flanked by a wave-built terrace. Shoreline elevations have generally been measured at the inflection point near the junction of the cut and fill parts of the terrace tread. Those in the main basin were cut into sandstone and were generally measured in the field with a barometric altimeter, using spot elevations at road junctions on topographic maps. Those in the Lewiston basin were cut into Pleistocene sediment and were picked from topographic maps with a 20-ft (6-m) contour interval. Shore terraces might be confused with stratigraphic benches in areas with Cambrian sandstone, especially in the southern end of the main basin and in adjacent smaller basins where the topographic benches on the Eau Claire Formation and at the top of the Wonewoc Formation are at the same elevation as the highest shoreline. Water levels based on shore terraces are probably typically within a few meters of the true values.

Shore deposits. Possible beach ridges have been recognized in several places, but those lacking exposures of beach sediment have not been plotted on the shore profiles—there is too great a likelihood for confusion with sand dunes. Several beach deposits, most of which have no associated recognizable beach ridge, have been plotted on the profiles shown in a later section. Most consist of gravel, with the cobbles of the softer lithologies being well rounded and disk shaped. In most places the cobbles consist primarily of well-cemented sandstone and concretions from the Cambrian formations and chert from the Ordovician Oneota Formation. Around Necedah Bluff, which was an island in the middle of the main basin, and around North Bluff, which was an island in the northwestern part of the main basin, the cobbles consist largely of hard Precambrian rock. Only those deposits that are unlikely to be fluvial sediment (because of inappropriate topographic position) or hillslope sediment (because the sandstone and concretion cobbles are too well rounded) have been plotted on the profiles. The elevations of most beach deposits were inter-

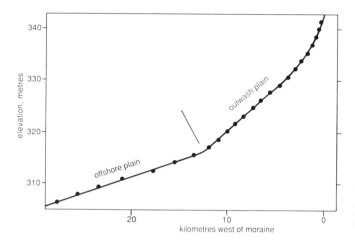

Figure 20. Topographic profile across outwash plain and offshore plain 10 km north of the village of Hancock, showing the break in slope (13 km west of the moraine) at the probable shoreline at 316 m (drawn from topographic maps with 5-ft contour intervals).

polated from topographic maps with 5-ft (1.5-m) contour intervals, and some are from maps with 10-ft (3-m) contour intervals or were measured with an altimeter. They are probably generally in error by no more than 1 or 2 m.

Ice-rafted erratics. The maximum elevation of scattered erratic boulders, cobbles, and pebbles on hillslopes has been plotted on the profiles in a few places. These elevations are derived from Alden (1918) and Martin (1916), who thought they indicated the maximum elevation of the lake. Alden and Martin's elevations were probably derived from topographic maps with 20-ft (6-m) contour intervals or were measured with an altimeter. They assumed that the erratics had been rafted into the lake basin on icebergs derived from the glacier to the east.

Offshore deposits. Offshore deposits are plotted on the shore profiles because the highest shorelines should occur above the highest offshore deposit. This material is discussed in more detail later. Only the elevations of the offshore silt and clay (not offshore sand because it could be confused with fluvial sand) have been plotted on the profiles. Some of these occurrences are outcrops; their elevations were largely derived from topographic maps with 5-ft (1.5-m) contour intervals and are likely to be within a few meters of the true values. Most occurrences, however, were noted in drill holes. Several hundred were noted in logs prepared by water-well drillers; individual elevations are likely to be within several meters of the true positions, but only clusters of well-documented occurrences are used, which are likely to be within only a few meters of the true elevations. A few hundred occurrences were also noted in logs of test holes reported by Harloff (1942); small clusters of these are apt to be within a few meters of the true elevations. Elevations reported in the individual test holes of Brownell (1986) are also likely to be within a few meters of the true values.

Break in slope. The east shore of the west Baraboo, Dell Creek, Hulburt, and main basins was the edge of the outwash plain west of the outer moraine of the Green Bay Lobe (Fig. 4). Along the southern part of this shoreline, west of the Johnstown

moraine, the outwash plain slopes westward more gently than the offshore face. The offshore face is a delta foreset face that has undergone later modification by wave erosion and still later modification by erosion during the draining of Lake Wisconsin.

In contrast, along the northern part of the shoreline, west of the Hancock moraine (Fig. 4), the outwash plain slopes westward at about 1.5 to 2 m/km to a break in slope, west of which the plain slopes westward at about 0.5 to 1 m/km (Fig. 20). The origin of this break in slope is unknown, and little information is available in this area on the location of the highest shoreline. However, when the break in slope is plotted on a shore profile, it corresponds to the highest shoreline extrapolated from farther south. Therefore, this break in slope is presumed to mark the shore at the time the outwash plain formed, and the break in slope is plotted on the shore profile as if it represents the shoreline. The break in slope was picked from topographic profiles constructed using topographic maps with 5-ft (1.5-m) contour intervals.

The interpretation of the break in slope as a shoreline feature is corroborated by the presence or absence of channel scars. Braided channel scars can be seen on aerial photographs in a few places on the outwash plain in Portage and Adams counties, but generally well above the break in slope. However, except on modern floodplains and on river terraces, no channel scars have been seen on the lake plain anywhere below the break in slope.

Shore-ice collapse trenches. On the outwash plain on the southeast side of the main basin in Adams County is a series of shallow trenches interpreted by Clayton and Attig (1987a) to be shore-ice collapse trenches (Figs. 21 and 22). They are about 1 m deep, 25 m wide, and as much as 2 km long, and they are oriented north-south, parallel to the shore of Lake Wisconsin.

These trenches are interpreted to have formed where shore ice was buried by outwash during the Johnstown Phase of glaciation; the outwash later collapsed to form the trenches when the ice melted. If this interpretation is correct, the ice was buried near lake level and the trenches formed above lake level. The elevation

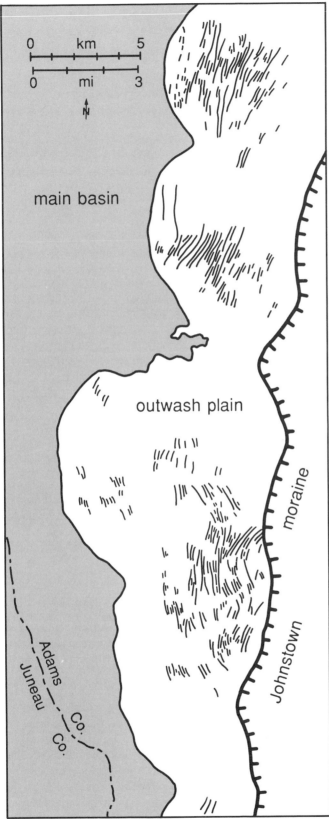

Figure 21. Map of shore-ice collapse trenches in southern Adams County (Clayton, 1987, Plate 1). The southern county boundary corresponds to the bottom edge of the map.

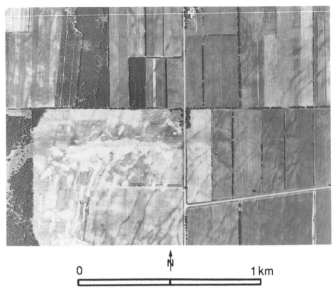

Figure 22. Aerial photograph of shore-ice collapse trenches (dark lines trending northeast-southwest). U.S. Department of Agriculture photograph AJA-1FF-186. Sec.25,T.15N.,R.6E., and Sec.30,T.15N.,R.7E., in the south-central part of the area shown in Figure 21.

of the ice and lake level is unknown, but the elevation of the trenches can be interpolated from topographic maps, which have 5-ft (1.5-m) contour intervals in this area. The trench elevations are therefore considered to indicate the maximum possible lake level in this area during the Johnstown Phase.

Shore cliffs and stacks. Shore cliffs are common along the shore of Lake Wisconsin, especially along the Wonewoc escarpment. Many are 30 m or more in height, with the entire stratigraphic sequence of the Wonewoc Formation exposed in their sides. They have not provided much useful information on lake levels, however, because the wave-cut platforms at the base of the cliffs are generally hidden under fans of debris eroded from the cliff during later higher water levels and during postlacustrine time.

A shore stack is a pinnacle of rock that has been detached from the main shore cliff by wave erosion. Black (1974, p. 137–150) has interpreted the bluffs in Figure 23 to be stacks. We know of no reason for thinking these bluffs were separated from the main shore cliff (just southwest of the area shown in Fig. 23) by wave erosion, however. Stacks are present, but they are generally too small to be individually shown on the 1:24,000 topographic maps. Some readily accessible examples are on the southeast side of Ragged Rock and south of Devils Monument (Fig. 23).

Shoreline-profile model

If the Earth's crust were stable, the shoreline data could be plotted on a simple elevation histogram, and clusters of data

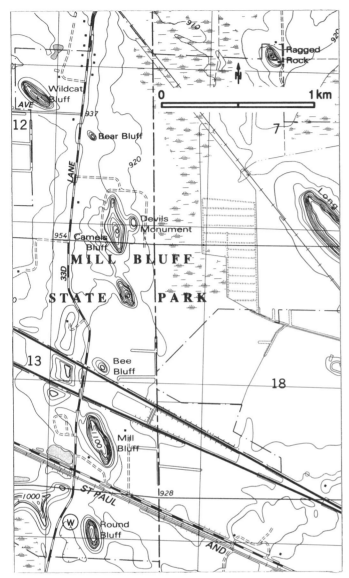

Figure 23. Topographic map of sandstone bluffs in Mill Bluff State Park (a unit of the Ice Age National Scientific Reserve), 4 km northwest of the village of Camp Douglas, in the western part of the main basin. The Johnstown shoreline was above the 900-ft (274-m) contour, and the Elderon shoreline was above the 940-ft (287-m) contour. The divided highway is Interstate 90 and 94. U.S. Geological Survey Camp Douglas Quadrangle (7.5 minute series; 20-ft contour interval; 1983).

points would indicate the position of shorelines. However, if we assume that the crust was depressed as a result of the weight of the glacier, the data must be plotted on a profile drawn parallel to the direction of crustal tilt. The nearest large mass of ice was to the northeast, so the crust should have tilted to the northeast when the weight of the ice was added, and it should have tilted back to the southwest when it was removed; the shoreline elevations therefore are plotted on a profile diagram oriented northeast-southwest (Fig. 24).

Assuming that no tilting occurred while the outlet was in use, that the tilt angle is uniform over the area, and that the outlet was not downcut while in use, a shore should plot as a straight line rising to the northeast or dropping to the southwest from an outlet (Fig. 24a, b, and c). If, however, tilting occurred while the outlet was in use, a series of shorelines would intersect at the outlet (Fig. 24d, e, and f). If no tilting occurred while the outlet was in use, but the outlet was downcut while in use, a series of parallel shorelines should result (Fig. 24g, h, and i). If tilting occurred while the outlet was in use and the outlet was downcut while in use, a series of shorelines would intersect some distance from the outlet (Fig. 24j, k, and l). If more than one outlet was used, a complex of confusingly intersecting shorelines might result, but fortunately the northwestern outlet functioned through nearly all of the history of the lake. If only scattered segments of the shorelines were preserved, as is true with Lake Wisconsin shorelines, there might be little chance of sorting out any but the highest ones. Therefore, attention is here focused on the highest shoreline in any area.

Which of these models best fits Lake Wisconsin? The northwest outlet was in use through most of Lake Wisconsin's

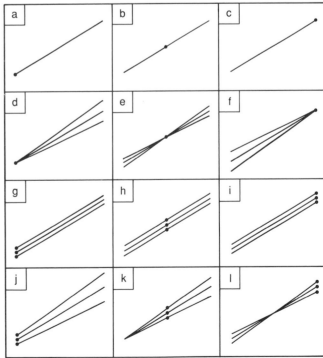

Figure 24. Hypothetical shoreline profiles resulting from various conditions mentioned in the text. Vertical axis is elevation; horizontal axis is distance (glacier to right). Dot is position of lake outlet.

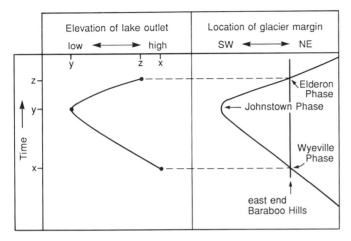

Figure 25. Hypothetical response of Earth's crust (left half of diagram) to weight of glacier advancing toward the southwest and melting back to the northeast (right half of diagram). Vertical axis is time.

history, so it is likely that considerable crustal tilt occurred while it was in use (Fig. 24d, e, f, j, k, and l). The northwest outlet was probably bottomed on resistant Precambrian rock, so it is unlikely that much downcutting occurred during use (Fig. 24d, e, and f). The northwest outlet was near the middle of the profile if crustal tilt was to the northeast, so Figure 24e seems a likely model for the highest Lake Wisconsin shore profile. Therefore, the highest shoreline in the northeastern part of the lake should be different from the highest shoreline in the southwestern part of the lake.

If there are two separate highest shorelines passing through the outlet as shown in Figure 24e, when might each have formed? As the Green Bay Lobe advanced into the area (right side of Fig. 25), the Earth's crust would begin to sink. Lake Wisconsin would come into existence when the glacier came to the Baraboo Hills. The elevation of the outlet would decrease from time x to time y (left side of Fig. 25), at which time the glacier began to waste back. The elevation of the outlet would then increase from y to z, when the lake would drain. Because there is a lag in the response of the crust to the weight of the ice, the outlet should have been slightly lower at the beginning (x) than at the end (z).

The events postulated in Figure 25 would result in the shore profile in Figure 26. Shoreline y, formed at the maximum glacial advance, would be steepest, and it would be the highest shoreline to the northeast of the outlet. Shoreline x would be the least steep of the shorelines formed while the northwest outlet was in use, and it would be the highest shoreline southwest of the outlet. For this reason, the highest shoreline in the northeast part of the main basin would have formed when the glacier stood at the Johnstown moraine, during the Johnstown Phase of glaciation, roughly 15,000 years ago (this chronology is discussed in more detail in a later section of this memoir). This hypothetical shoreline will here be referred to as the Johnstown shoreline. Little is known about the details of glaciation before the Johnstown Phase. During the Wisconsin Glaciation, it seems likely that the Green Bay Lobe reached the Baraboo Hills for the first time roughly 19,000 years ago; this event will here be called the Wyeville Phase, named after a community in the southwestern part of the main basin. The hypothetical shoreline formed then, which should be the highest shoreline to the southwest of the northwest outlet, will be referred to as the Wyeville shoreline.

Neither the Wyeville nor the Johnstown shorelines should be present in the basins east of the Johnstown moraine (Fig. 4) because these basins were occupied by the glacier until after the Johnstown Phase. Therefore, shoreline z (Fig. 26) should be the highest shoreline in the east Baraboo basin and in that part of the

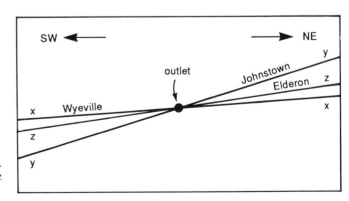

Figure 26. Shoreline profiles resulting from conditions in Figure 25. Vertical axis is elevation; horizontal axis is distance. Shorelines x, y, and z correspond to times and elevations x, y, and z of Figure 25.

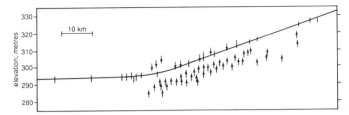

Lewiston basin south of the line of no tilt drawn through the northwest outlet of the main basin. Because the lake drained during the Elderon Phase of glaciation, roughly 14,000 years ago, this hypothetical shoreline will here be referred to as the Elderon shoreline.

Shoreline profiles

Based on scanty information on the highest shorelines in the northern part of the main basin, and assuming uniform tilt, Martin (1916, p. 320) suggested that the shorelines rise to the north at a rate of about 0.06 to 0.13 m/km. Martin also suggested as an alternative that the shorelines might be horizontal in the southern part of the lake, with shorelines in the northern part (north of a "hinge line") rising to the north at about 0.25 m/km. However, Hadley and Pelham (1976), on their map of the Pleistocene deposits of Wisconsin, drew the outline of Lake Wisconsin everywhere at the 1,000-ft (305-m) contour, as if there had been no crustal tilt.

As indicated in the previous section, it seems most likely that the shorelines rise to the northeast. This is borne out by the shoreline observations. A line for the shore profile was picked by

Figure 27. First trial shoreline profile, assuming that the direction of crustal tilt was the same for all shorelines (S60°W). Vertical dashes are elevations of shore terraces, shore deposits, and breaks in slope at foot of outwash plain. Downward pointing arrows are elevations of shore-ice-collapse trenches and meander scars. Upward pointing arrows are offshore silt deposits.

determining a line of no tilt through the northwest outlet. First the approximate elevation of water at the northwest outlet was determined. The highest shoreline elevations along the southeast shore were then scanned for an equivalent elevation. A line of no tilt was drawn between these two points. A line perpendicular to this line of no tilt was used for the first trial shore profile, which was oriented N60°E (Fig. 27).

The result of the first trial profile showed a rather sharp bend at the position of the northwest outlet (Fig. 27). The rate of crustal tilt with distance might not be uniform, as assumed in Figure 24, but the profile would be expected to curve gently rather than bend sharply. This indicates that, as predicted, the profile does correspond to the model suggested in Figure 24e. It seems likely therefore that the shoreline southwest of the outlet is the Wyeville shoreline, and the one northeast of the outlet is the Johnstown shoreline. Because the crustal tilt directions might be different at different times, the Johnstown, Wyeville, and Elderon shorelines were plotted separately on the final profiles (shown in Figs. 28, 30, and 32).

Johnstown shoreline. The Johnstown shoreline, as reconstructed here, has been tilted about S60°W at about 0.7 m/km. Most of the elevations plotted on the shore profile (Fig. 28) come

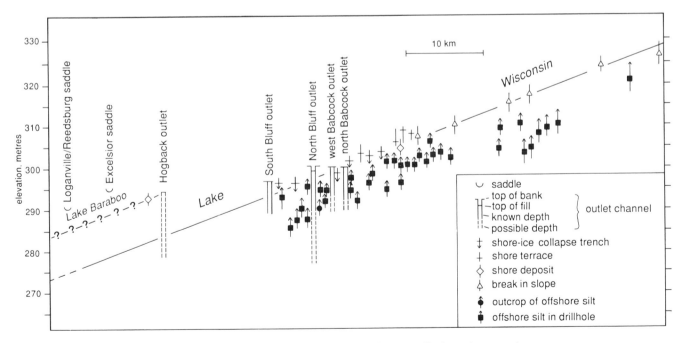

Figure 28. The Johnstown shoreline profile; oriented S60°W, perpendicular to the water-plane contours shown in Figure 29. Vertical bars indicate range of likely elevations for each point.

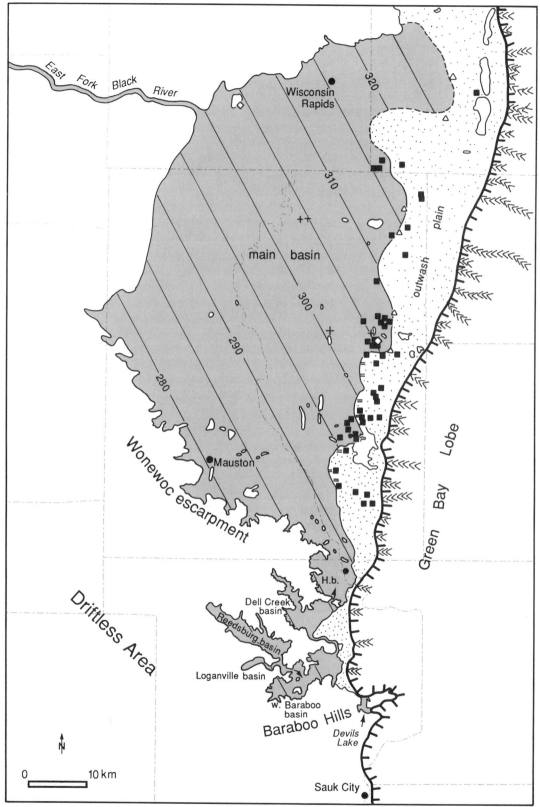

Figure 29. Map of Lake Wisconsin during the Johnstown Phase. The glacier margin is shown as a line with tick marks. The nested arrow heads show the position of tunnel channels. The contour lines show elevation of water plane above present sea level in meters. Spot symbols are same as in Figure 28. H.b.: Hulburt basin.

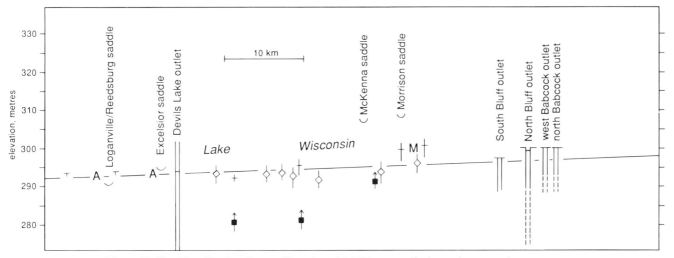

Figure 30. The Wyeville shoreline profile; oriented S45°E, perpendicular to the water-plane contours shown in Figure 31. Same symbols as in Figure 28, with the following exceptions. T: Lowest river terraces formed before the last part of the Wisconsin Glaciation, in the southwestern part of Juneau County. A: Highest ice-rafted erratics reported by Alden (1918). M: Highest ice-rafted erratics reported by Martin (1916).

from the west edge of the outwash plain west of the Johnstown moraine (Fig. 29), so it seems unlikely that this shoreline formed before the Johnstown Phase of the Wisconsin Glaciation.

The elevation of the Johnstown shoreline in the northwest part of the main basin is based primarily on the outlet elevation and on the elevation of an isolated shore deposit (Fig. 29; southeast corner of Sec.28,T.22N.,R.4E.). The shore deposit was well exposed in a new gravel pit. It is made up of shingled gravel consisting of well-rounded, disk-shaped sandstone fragments. Its elevation was determined from a contour map with a 5-ft (1.5-m) contour interval, supplemented with altimeter measurements.

The highest shore terrace plotted on Figure 28 seems to be too high. It may actually be a stratigraphic bench, or it may represent an earlier shoreline. Alternatively, it may be a Johnstown shore terrace that is high because it is from an island near the middle of the lake where some additional crustal rebound occurred when the weight of the lake water was released, whereas most other elevations are from near the margins of the basin where thick lake sediment underwent some compaction, causing lower elevations.

Which of the northwest outlets were used at this time is unclear, but the north Babcock outlet (Figs. 5, 28, and 29) seems to have been the lowest then and therefore is the most likely. The lowest outlet from the Reedsburg, Loganville, and west Baraboo basins (Fig. 29) was the Hogback outlet (Fig. 28). The Excelsior saddle was at least a few meters higher. If the Hogback outlet had a nearly flat gradient, the water in the basins upstream from the Hogback outlet can be considered part of Lake Wisconsin. However, if the outlet had become superimposed on resistant rock, it is possible that the water dropped a few meters through the outlet.

If so, the water in the basins upstream from the Hogback outlet at that time can be considered to be a separate Lake Baraboo.

Delta foreset beds were reported in 1923 in two gravel pits at the east end of the Baraboo basin; the pits are at the west edge of the outwash plain, about 1 km southwest of the Baraboo outlet (locations 41 and 42 of Road Material Investigation Report 316, in the files of the Wisconsin Geological and Natural History Survey). The tops of the foreset beds are roughly 10 m above the level of Lake Wisconsin. Therefore, Lake Baraboo is tentatively shown 10 m above Lake Wisconsin in Figure 28.

When the lake stood at the Johnstown shoreline, the water was only a few meters deep in much of the northwestern, northern, and northeastern parts of the main basin, deepening to about 25 m in the south-central part. The water gradually deepened to about 15 m in the down-valley parts of the Reedsburg and west Baraboo basins, to about 10 m in the south-central part of the Dell Creek basin, and to about 6 m in the down-valley part of the Loganville basin. The water was probably a few meters deep in much of the Hulburt basin.

Wyeville shoreline. The Wyeville shoreline, as reconstructed here, has been tilted about S45°W, at about 6 cm/km. The elevations shown on the shore profile (Fig. 30) are primarily from beach deposits scattered throughout the southwestern part of the main basin (Fig. 31). The lowest northwest outlet at this time was probably the South Bluff outlet. The water in the Reedsburg basin flowed to the rest of Lake Wisconsin through the Upper Narrows outlet, not through the Excelsior saddle, which was probably a few meters too high at this time.

It is possible, but not probable, that the shoreline shown in Figure 30 is not the Wyeville shoreline—that is, it did not form

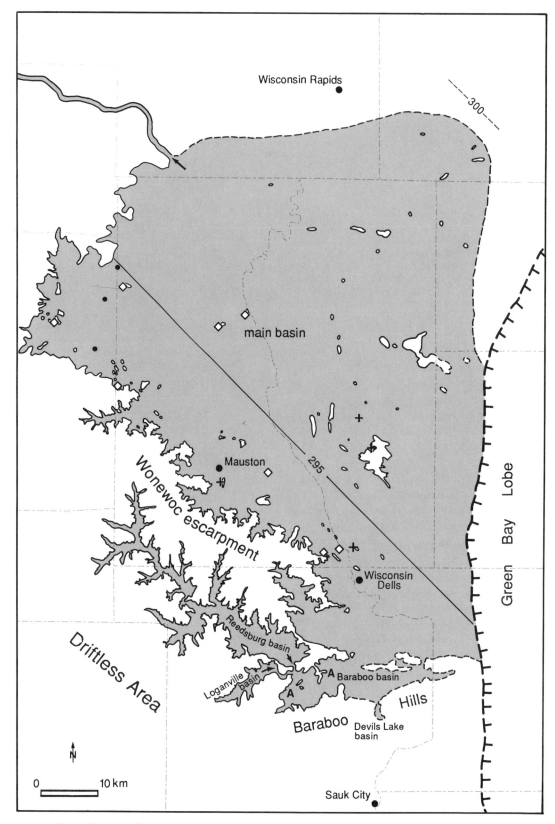

Figure 31. Map of Lake Wisconsin during the Wyeville Phase. Same symbols as in Figure 29. The details along the eastern and northern sides are poorly known.

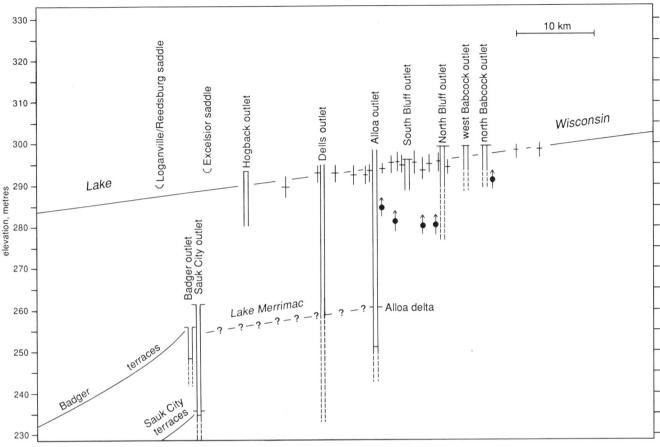

Figure 32. The Elderon shoreline profile; oriented N55°E, perpendicular to the water-plane contours shown in Figure 33. Same symbols as in Figure 28.

when the glacier was at the east end of the Baraboo Hills. Instead it might have formed when the glacier was at Devils Nose southeast of Devils Lake (Fig. 19). If the Devils Lake gorge was blocked with till above an elevation of about 293 m, Lake Wisconsin would have risen to the level of the northwest outlet (about 293 m) when the glacier reached the east end of the Baraboo Hills; but if it was not blocked, Lake Wisconsin would have been at the level of the Devils Lake outlet, below the Wyeville level, until the glacier reached Devils Nose. There is no direct evidence that the Devils Lake outlet was blocked at this time. However, the gradient of the shoreline reconstructed here is more similar to that of the Elderon shoreline than it is to that of the Johnstown shoreline. Therefore, it seems likely that the glacial margin at this time was closer to the Elderon margin than to the Johnstown margin. For this reason, it seems more likely that the Wyeville shoreline as shown in Fig. 30 is the result of an ice dam at the east end of the Baraboo Hills than one at Devils Nose. This requires that the Devils Lake gorge was filled with till above an elevation of 293 m before the last part of the Wisconsin Glaciation.

There is little evidence of the position of the glacier margin during Wyeville time, so it is roughly indicated on Figure 31 at about the position of the Elderon glacier margin. The location of the eastern shore, and especially the northeastern shore, of the lake in Wyeville time is unclear because the thickness of sediment deposited after Wyeville time, and therefore the elevation of the land surface during Wyeville time, is unclear.

When Lake Wisconsin stood at the Wyeville shoreline, the water was roughly 30 m deep in the south-central part of the main basin, at least 30 m and 24 m deep in the Reedsburg and Loganville basins, probably around 45 m deep in the east end of the Baraboo basin, and more than 50 m deep in the southeast part of the Lewiston basin, where the present floodplain of the Wisconsin River is that far below the Wyeville shoreline.

Elderon shoreline. The Elderon shoreline has been tilted about S50° or 55°W, at about 0.2 m/km. The elevations used to reconstruct the profile shown in Figure 32 are mostly from shore terraces in the Lewiston basin (Fig. 33). The single elevation from the northwestern part of the lake is from the northwest outlet. The specific northwest outlet used at this time is uncertain, and

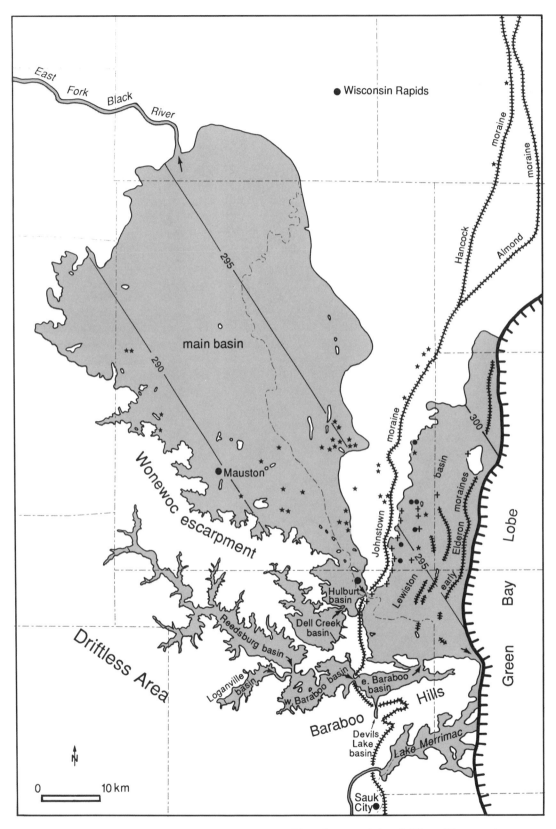

Figure 33. Map of Lake Wisconsin during the Elderon Phase. Same symbols as in Figure 29, except that the lines with cross bars west of the glacier represent end moraines, and the stars indicate groups of ice-wedge polygons.

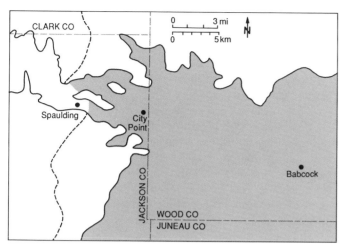

Figure 34. The present-day 990-ft (302-m) contour in the northwestern part of the main basin, near the elevation of a pre-Wyeville shoreline. Gray area is approximate location of Lake Wisconsin. Dashed line is preglacial drainage divide. Same area as Figure 5.

the elevation of the water surface in the northwest outlets is rather imprecisely known. Therefore, the direction of shoreline tilt is imprecisely known. The North Bluff outlet is shown being used in Figure 33 because it is the freshest looking of the northwest outlets, still retaining a shallow channel form.

The water from the Reedsburg, Loganville, east Baraboo, and west Baraboo basins drained through the Lower Narrows outlet to the Lewiston basin at this time. Both the Excelsior and Hogback saddles were a few meters above lake level at this time. Water flowed westward from the Lewiston basin to the Hulburt and main basins through the Dells outlet.

The glacier margin shown in Figure 33, just as the lake was beginning to drain, probably does not correspond to any recognized moraine, because the ice margin should have been actively retreating when drainage occurred. To the west of this ice margin, a moraine occurs at Briggsville in southwestern Marquette County, another occurs 3 km east of the moraine at Briggsville, and another occurs 1 km to the west of Briggsville (Fig. 33). These three moraines probably correlate with older Elderon moraines in Portage County (Clayton, 1986) and Marathon County (Attig and Muldoon, 1989). These moraines in the Lewiston basin have wave-planed crests, indicating that Lake Wisconsin continued to exist after they formed. Just to the east of the ice margin shown in Figure 33 is a moraine that lacks a wave-planed crest; correlation northward is uncertain, but this is equivalent to one of the younger Elderon moraines. That is, Lake Wisconsin drained during the middle or late part of the Elderon Phase of glaciation.

When Lake Wisconsin stood at the Elderon shoreline, water was only a few meters deep in much of northwestern, northern, and northeastern parts of the main basin, deepening to about 27 m in the south-central part. The water deepened down valley to about 26, 21, 42, and 19 m in the Reedsburg, west Baraboo, east Baraboo, and Loganville basins, respectively, and was about 22 m deep in the south-central part of the Dell Creek basin. The lake was deepest in the southeastern part of the Lewiston basin, where

the present floodplain of the Wisconsin River is 50 m below the Elderon shoreline.

Pre-Wyeville shorelines. The Wyeville shoreline shown in Figure 30 was reconstructed using the highest observations of shore elevations from the southwestern part of the lake, with five exceptions. These five observations were not used because they are too high for any lake that could have existed when the configuration of the landscape at the northwest outlet was similar to the configuration seen there today. The outlet used during the last part of the Wisconsin Glaciation preserves a clear channel form in Jackson County where not buried by later sediment (Figs. 5 and 7). There the channel has a uniform width of about 0.5 km. Two of these five observations were made near the northwest outlet and indicate a shoreline near 302 m. If the lake had been at 302 m during the last part of the Wisconsin Glaciation, the outlet would have been a strait about 2 km wide across the drainage divide at Spaulding (Figs. 5 and 34), 20 km downstream from the present drainage divide. It is unlikely that any outlet would have been 2 km wide; more likely it was about 0.5 km wide, as it was during the last lake episode. Furthermore, no channel form exists at 302 m. This indicates that a considerable amount of erosion has occurred since the lake was at that level, and it indicates that the lake was at that level well before the Spaulding and later outlets were cut—that is, well before the last part of the Wisconsin Glaciation. Therefore, this shoreline is considered to be a pre-Wyeville shoreline, formed perhaps during the early part of the Wisconsin Glaciation or more likely before the Wisconsin Glaciation.

Three of these five observations were derived from beach deposits near the northwest outlet. One occurs on the northwest side of North Bluff at UTM coordinates YV2473-1173. It consists of a spit of rounded gravel, made of Precambrian rock derived from North Bluff, between the 990-ft and 995-ft (302-m and 303-m) contours. Two other deposits occur 3 km east of City Point between the 990-ft and 995-ft (302-m and 303-m) contours (UTM coordinates YV1656-1455) and on the 985-ft (300-m) contour (YV1602-1286); both consist of rounded and shingled sandstone gravel.

A fourth shore deposit occurs 5 km west of Wyeville at UTM coordinates YU0456-7730. It consists of flat-bedded forebeach sediment overlying foreset beds of the wave-built terrace; the probable water level was measured with an altimeter to be about 300 m. If this pre-Wyeville shoreline has been tilted the same direction and amount as the Wyeville shoreline, it should now be 2 m lower here than near the northwest outlet, making it equivalent to the 302-m shoreline suggested in the previous paragraph.

The fifth deposit consists of 6 m of horizontally bedded offshore silt 9 km southwest of Lyndon Station at UTM coordinates YU6010-3703, in the upper part of Dell Creek valley. The top of the deposit is at an elevation of 302 m, measured with a level from a nearby spot elevation of 296.6 m on the U.S. Geological Survey's Lyndon Station Quadrangle (7.5 minute, topographic). The water level was probably at least 3 m deep, so the lake level was probably over 305 m. If the shoreline tilt was similar to that of the Wyeville beach, it should now be 2 m lower here than near the northwest outlet, making it at least 5 m above the 302-m shoreline suggested in the previous paragraphs. Therefore, the shoreline tilt was quite different from that during the Wyeville Phase, or the silt was deposited in an even earlier lake. Alternatively, this deposit may be unrelated to Lake Wisconsin but instead might have been deposited in a lake dammed in the Dell Creek valley by a landslide. Such a landslide would have had to occur no more than 3 km downstream, where the valley widens, but no evidence of any appropriate landslide is known.

Precision. The elevations in Figures 28, 30, and 32 are shown with vertical bars, giving a rough estimate of the probable range of true position. This judgement was made for each elevation on the basis of a variety of factors, including the uncertainty in locating a feature on a topographic map, the lateral and elevational precision of the topographic maps used, various uncertainties in well-log depths, and uncertainties in interpretation of lake level with respect to the observed field feature.

The water plane on each of these figures is represented by a line. The actual water plane was probably within 2 m of this line in areas of abundant data.

Accuracy. The shorelines described in the preceding paragraphs are based on scanty information, and therefore some comments are required on the possibility of major errors in their reconstruction. Because some trial-and-error experimentation was required, there was a possibility of circular reasoning. The shoreline-elevation observations had to be assigned to the correct profle (Wyeville, Johnstown, or Elderon), and these observations were in turn used to determine the tilt direction for each profile. In addition, there was some danger of self-fulfilling hypotheses. Field work continued as the various trials were made, so there is the possibility that inadequate information was collected where no shorelines were predicted by the early trial.

Another potential source of confusion is the glacial advance-and-retreat model shown on the right-hand side of Figure 25; the glacier is known to have undergone shorter-term fluctuations not shown in this diagram. For example, the Elderon Phase is known to have involved several small advances and retreats of the ice margin. Some of these fluctuations might have been large enough to affect the shape of the elevation curve shown in the left-hand part of Figure 25.

Nevertheless, the Wyeville, Johnstown, and Elderon shorelines, as reconstructed here, probably represent actual shorelines. By using only the highest shoreline observations in any area, confusion resulting from the overlapping of lower shorelines is largely avoided. The reconstructed Elderon shoreline is free of any confusion caused by inclusion of Johnstown or Wyeville observations because any Wyeville shoreline features east of the Johnstown moraine would have been destroyed by the glacial advance to the moraine, and Johnstown shoreline features were only formed west of the moraine. Some Johnstown and Wyeville observations may have been confused with each other in the area where the two shorelines cross, but a large number of the observations are far enough from the crossing area that little confusion is likely.

An additional possible problem is the shape of the profile lines. The tilted shore profiles of large glacial lakes such as the Great Lakes are known to curve (see, for example, Larsen, 1987), but for a profile only 80 km long, the curve is likely to deviate no more than a few meters from a straight line, which is close to the precision range of the profiles shown here.

A test of these shoreline reconstructions has been provided by Guetter and Clark (Guetter, Clark, and Clayton, 1987). Their predictions indicate the shorelines of Lake Wisconsin when it first came into existence during the last part of the Wisconsin Glaciation (Wyeville), when the glacier was at its maximum position (Johnstown), and when it finally drained (Elderon). Their predictions were based on a "numerical model of a spherically symmetric viscoelastic earth." The direction and amount of tilt of the predicted and observed shorelines are shown in Table 1.

The Guetter and Clark predictions and the Clayton and Attig observations shown in Table 1 were made independently of each other, with no chance of the results of one influencing the other. The reconstructed tilt rates are nearly the same as the theoretical tilt rates, which tends to substantiate the reconstructed shorelines. The reconstructed tilt directions are 15° more westerly than the theoretical tilt directions, perhaps because of a thinner, more dynamic ice sheet than assumed in the model.

OFFSHORE SEDIMENT

The distribution of Lake Wisconsin offshore sediment is shown in Figure 35. Cross sections through this material are given by Clayton (1986, 1987, 1989a, 1989b), Clayton and Attig (Sauk County report, in preparation), and Brownell (1986). The Pleistocene sediment, most of which is probably offshore sediment, is a few tens of meters thick in many parts of the main basin (Fig. 36); it is as thick as 60 m in some places in the southeast; and it is generally only a few meters thick along the western side

**TABLE 1. ORIENTATION OF WATER PLANES PREDICTED BY
GUETTER AND CLARK AND
OBSERVED BY CLAYTON AND ATTIG**

	Wyeville	Johnstown	Elderon
Guetter and Clark	S30°W 0.17 m/km	S45°W 0.53 m/km	S40°W 0.38 m/km
This memoir	S45°W 0.06 m/km	S60°W 0.7 m/km	S50-55°W 0.2 m/km
Clayton and Attig (1987b)	S45°W 0.1 m/km	S60°W 0.6 m/km	S55°W 0.3 m/km

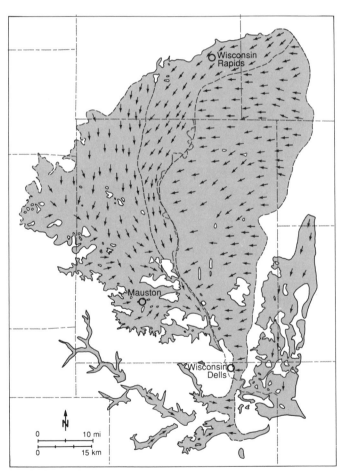

Figure 35. Map showing areas of offshore sediment deposited in Lake Wisconsin. The dashed lines in the main basin show the contacts between offshore sediment from the Yellow and Lemonweir Rivers and tributaries (west side), offshore sediment from the Wisconsin River (middle), and offshore sediment from the Johnstown outwash plain (east). Arrows indicate general direction of meltwater movement.

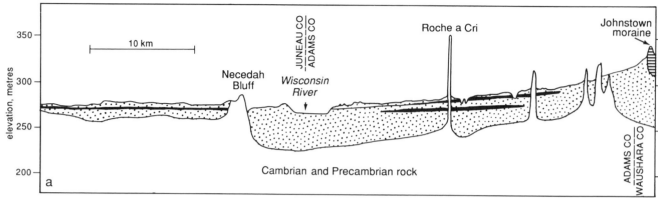

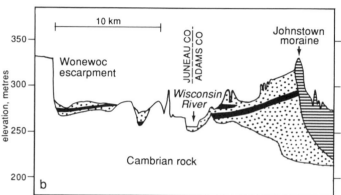

Figure 36. East-west cross sections through Lake Wisconsin off-shore deposits. Black area is offshore silt; upper bed is the New Rome Member. Dotted area is sand (largely offshore sand below 300 m). In western Adams County the sand over the New Rome Member is largely windblown. Horizontally ruled area is till of the Johnstown moraine. From Clayton (1987; 1989b). a: South half of T.18N., in the middle of the main basin. b: North half of T.14N., in the southern part of the main basin.

of the main basin. It is a few tens of meters thick in parts of the Lewiston basin. In the southern basins west of the Johnstown moraine, the thickness of Pleistocene sediment generally increases down valley to about 65 m near the moraine; probably over half of this is offshore sediment.

Offshore silt in main basin

The offshore silt of Lake Wisconsin is clearly identifiable in most places because it is commonly distinctly laminated, but only about a tenth of the offshore sediment deposited in the main basin is silt, the bulk of it being sand. Most of the observed silt is part of the New Rome Member of the Horicon and Big Flats Formations.

The New Rome Member was named by Brownell (in Attig and others, 1989a) for the former community of New Rome in northwestern Adams County. The New Rome Member occurs throughout most of the main basin. The distribution of the New Rome Member is known from the logs of several hundred forest-fire protection wells (Harloff, 1942) and water wells (in Wisconsin Geological and Natural History Survey files) as well as from the logs of wells drilled by Brownell (1986). It has also been observed in several dozen exposures in road cuts, borrow pits, reservoir cutbanks, and the sides of small valleys.

The New Rome Member is typically 0.5 to 5 m thick. It is buried under several meters of offshore sand in most places but is

near the surface in a large part of west-central Adams County where wind erosion has removed the overlying sand (Fig. 36). It is most deeply buried in the northeast part of the basin, where it is overlain by 18 m of offshore sediment, and just west of the Johnstown moraine in Adams County, where it is overlain by 25 m of offshore and stream sand. The sediment is generally reddish brown but is brown or gray in some places. In many places it is rhythmically laminated, probably varved. According to Brownell (in Attig and others, 1989a), it typically consists of about half silt, a quarter clay, and a quarter very fine sand. About a fifth of the coarse silt is dolomite; the New Rome silt was once mined in this area as a source of agricultural lime.

The New Rome silt bed is underlain in most places by sand, probably primarily offshore sand. One or more beds of silt occur under the sand under the New Rome bed in a few places, but little is known about them. An example, in central Adams County, is shown in Figure 36a.

Offshore sand in main basin

East of the Wisconsin River. The sediment deposited in the main basin east of the Wisconsin River has been included in the Big Flats Formation by Brownell (in Attig and others, 1989a). Most of it consists of sand deposited by meltwater that came directly from the Green Bay Lobe to the east (Figs. 29 and 35). The meltwater flowed westward out of the glacier across 5 or 10 km of outwash plain, entered the lake, and continued westward 10 or 20 km to the deep part of the lake, near the present Wisconsin River.

The great bulk of the sediment deposited in the main basin was sand rather than silt or clay because most of the sediment fed into the basin was sand. The meltwater, when it was beneath the glacier, had access to till, which consisted of roughly 85 percent sand, 5 percent gravel, 5 percent silt, and 5 percent clay, in addition to older Pleistocene stream deposits, which consisted of slightly gravelly sand and Cambrian sand and sandstone (Figs. 2 and 3). The load of the rivers debouching onto the outwash plain was therefore probably around nine-tenths sand. Like the sand in the Cambrian formations to the northeast of the lake, the offshore sand is predominantly well-rounded medium sand composed of quartz. Nearly all of the gravel load and part of the sand load was dropped in the outwash plain before it reached the lake; the lake sand rarely has as much as 1 percent gravel in it.

The sand in the main basin east of the present Wisconsin River is interpreted to be lake sand rather than river sand for the following reasons. The sand east of the Wisconsin River is known to have been deposited by meltwater flowing westward from the Green Bay Lobe because the land surface slopes westward from the Johnstown moraine to the Wisconsin River. The Johnstown moraine is presently the drainage divide between the Wisconsin River valley to the west and the Fox River valley to the east (Fig. 36b). Once the ice melted back about 3 km east of the Johnstown moraine, not quite to the oldest Elderon moraine, the meltwater flowed southward between the Johnstown moraine and the glacier into the north end of the Lewiston basin. The glacier had to melt back an additional several kilometers, to near the youngest Elderon moraine, before the lake drained (Fig. 33). Therefore, the sand deposited between the modern Wisconsin River and the eastern edge of the main basin must have been deposited while the lake was in existence, and therefore the sand below lake level must be lake sediment (with the exception of a small amount of sediment deposited on the floodplains of small postglacial streams, and also with the exception of the windblown sand at the surface). This interpretation is substantiated by the presence of braided channel scars on the outwash plain and their absence on the lake plain.

The lake sand that was deposited at and just below the position of the Johnstown shoreline along the east side of the main basin as shown in Figure 29 is probably largely shoreline sand, but it is too poorly exposed to confirm this interpretation. The lake sand more than a few meters below the Johnstown level is interpreted to be offshore sand, but few exposures were observed, and there is little sedimentologic evidence for or against this interpretation.

How was this offshore sand carried into the east side of the main basin? Density currents seem the only currents likely to have flowed fast enough to have carried sand 10 to 20 km into the lake. Most of the sand of the outwash plain between the Johnstown shore and the Johnstown moraine is in the form of low fans with their apexes at the mouths of tunnel channels (Fig.

37). The tunnel channels were cut under the glacier by periodic outbreaks of huge volumes of meltwater (Clayton, 1986, p. 10; Wright, 1973). The tunnel channels were typically 0.5 km wide and perhaps 10 or 20 m deep. By the time this water reached the lake it had probably spread to a width of a few kilometers and thinned to a depth of a few meters. The offshore plain now slopes westward at about 0.5 to 1 m/km, but it was less steep before the post-Johnstown crustal tilt occurred. This mass of cold and turbid—and therefore heavy—water flowed down the offshore plain as an underflow current, carrying the sand as bedload out into the lake. The break in slope at the shoreline, from about 1.5 to 2 m/km on the outwash plain to about 0.5 to 1.0 m/km on the offshore plain, may indicate that the current increased in velocity as it entered the lake. The increased drag at the upper surface of the flow (against air where it was on the outwash plain but against lake water where it was on the offshore plain) was perhaps more than compensated for by the decreased drag as a result of a change from a braided channel on the outwash plain to a more continuous sheet of water on the lake bed.

West of the Wisconsin River. Most of the sand deposited in the middle of the main basin west of the present Wisconsin River was deposited by meltwater brought from northern Wisconsin by the Wisconsin River (Fig. 35). Its load consisted of material derived not only from beneath the glacier in northern Wisconsin but also from a variety of Precambrian and Pleistocene material exposed in cutbanks of the meltwater rivers in central Wisconsin. In addition, some sand was washed into the west edge of the lake by nonmeltwater rivers such as the Yellow and Lemonweir and their tributaries, and much of the surface sand in the western half of the basin was deposited by modern rivers after the lake drained. Throughout the basin the upper part of the offshore sand has been reworked by wind; dunes as high as 20 m occur in some places (Clayton, 1987).

The offshore sand west of the Wisconsin River is harder to interpret because there is the possibility of confusion with stream sediment. East of the river, meltwater streams ceased flowing well before the lake drained, so the material below the Johnstown shoreline has to be lake sediment, but west of the river there is the possibility that the material under the south-sloping plain next to the Wisconsin River (Fig. 35) was deposited by the Wisconsin River after the lake drained. Terraces underlain by stream sediment are present along the Wisconsin River. The highest (Love terrace) is interpreted to have formed when the glacier stood at the Winegar moraine in northern Wisconsin, after the lake drained (Clayton, 1986, 1987, 1989a, 1989b). It is clearly a stream terrace, with a braided channel pattern on its surface; it is underlain by sand containing several percent gravel. The surface immediately above this terrace, however, is underlain by sand interpreted to be offshore sediment deposited by underflow currents introduced into the lake by the Wisconsin River because it resembles the sand interpreted to be offshore sediment on the east side of the river. Like the offshore plain east of the river, the one west of the river lacks meltwater-stream channel scars, and it lacks the gravel present in the sand of the river terraces. Like the

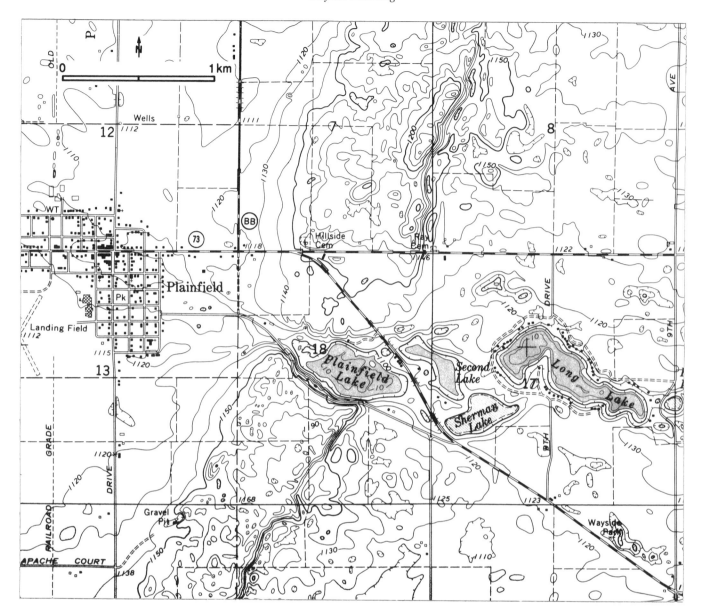

Figure 37. Tunnel channel (occupied by the Plainfield chain of lakes) breaching the Hancock moraine (within the 1,150-ft contour), with a fan of outwash beyond the mouth of the channel (west of the moraine). U.S. Geological Survey Plainfield Quadrangle (7.5 minute series; 10-ft contour interval; 1968). The village of Plainfield is in northwestern Waushara County (Fig. 1), T.20N.,R.8E.

offshore sand east of the river, that west of it was also probably deposited during periodic large-volume outbursts of meltwater; like the Johnstown moraine, the outer moraines of north-central Wisconsin are also breached by tunnel channels.

To the west of the south-sloping plain along the Wisconsin River (Fig. 35) is a plain that slopes south and southeast along the Yellow and Lemonweir Rivers and their tributaries. None of these rivers carried meltwater during the last part of the Wisconsin Glaciation. Tens of meters of sand occurs under the eastern part of this surface, but much of it is probably a buried part of Wisconsin River offshore fan. The material near the surface (but below the surface windblown sand), however, had its source in the Yellow and Lemonweir drainage basins because the surface slopes are parallel to these rivers and their tributaries rather than to the Wisconsin River. Much of it is probably offshore sediment rather than river sediment because it lacks channel scars. Some of this sand was probably introduced into the lake during spring melt where sand had blown out onto the lake ice.

The Lewiston sand trap

As much as 15 m of offshore sand overlies about 3 m of New Rome silt in the eastern part of the main basin, and as much as a few tens of meters of offshore sand underlies it. The top and bottom of the silt bed are generally sharply defined, indicating a sudden shift from sand deposition to silt deposition back to sand deposition. The causes of these shifts in sedimentation are unknown but may be related to a sand trap in the Lewiston basin.

The New Rome silt bed was deposited in the main basin on a surface that gradually rises eastward to near the position of the Johnstown moraine (Fig. 36b). Eastward from there the land drops steeply into the Lewiston basin. That is, a submerged ridge already separated the Lewiston and main basins. Because Johnstown outwash overlies the New Rome silt, the silt had to have been deposited before the Johnstown Phase. As the Green Bay Lobe advanced westward before the Johnstown Phase, it moved into the Lewiston basin. Meltwater from the glacier would have lost its bed load in deltas along the east side of the Lewiston basin, but the silt could have been washed through the basin over the submerged ridge to the main basin, where it was deposited. The Lewiston basin would cease to function as a sand trap when the ice reached the submerged ridge, and sand would begin to be deposited on top of the silt in the main basin. Sometime before the Johnstown Phase, as sand was built up, the submerged ridge became a peninsula and then an isthmus. By the time the glacier melted back far enough to again expose the Lewiston basin, the isthmus had completely separated the two basins, except for the narrow Dells outlet (Fig. 4). This constriction probably only allowed relatively warm and clear surface water to flow from the Lewiston basin to the main basin, and as a result the sand above the New Rome silt was not overlain by another silt layer when the sand trap began to function again in post-Johnstown time.

This interpretation applies only to the New Rome silt east of the Wisconsin River, where the silt came from the east, out of the Lewiston basin. A bed of silt much like the New Rome bed, which Brownell (1986) has correlated with the New Rome bed, occurs west of the Wisconsin River, in the fan of lake sediment brought from the north by the Wisconsin River. It is unclear if the supply of sand to the Wisconsin River in northern Wisconsin was cut off for a time, and it is unknown if that time coincided with the time of the Lewiston sand trap.

Offshore sediment in other basins

Thick offshore silt and clay occurs in parts of the Lewiston basin. In southeastern Adams County it is typically 5 to 25 m thick, is reddish brown or gray, and overlies sand (Clayton, 1987). This material is much younger than the New Rome Member.

Much of the 100 m of Pleistocene sand in the Devils Lake basin may be offshore sediment deposited when it was connected to Lake Wisconsin. Silt and clay are described at depths of 68 to 96 m in logs of wells drilled just above the level of modern Devils Lake (Wisconsin Geological and Natural History Survey Geologic Logs Sk-14 and Sk-15).

The Reedsburg, Dell Creek, and Loganville basins and the east and west Baraboo basins contain as much as 30 m of offshore silt and clay in addition to about an equivalent amount of sand, much of which is probably offshore sediment. The silt and clay is generally reddish brown in basins receiving considerable meltwater from the glacier, but in the southwestern basins it is generally gray.

FINAL DRAINAGE

The configuration of Lake Wisconsin just as it finally began to drain is shown in Figures 32, 33, and 38. The probable nature of the final drainage event has been previously described (Clayton and Attig, 1987b), but some aspects of it are further discussed here.

The final drainage can perhaps best be visualized by comparing it with better-known drainage events of other glacial lakes. One of the best-known modern drainage events occurred at the Hubbard Glacier in Yakutat Bay in southeastern Alaska (Emery and Seitz, 1987). The Hubbard Glacier had moved across Russell Fiord and up onto Gilbert Point on the other side of the fiord, damming a lake in the fiord. This lake was about a third the size of the Lewiston basin of Lake Wisconsin. The geometry of the glacial dam at Gilbert Point was very similar to that of the Green Bay Lobe on the east end of the Baraboo Hills. The lake surface was 25 m above sea level, a little less than the height of Lake Wisconsin above Lake Merrimac. On October 7 and 8, 1986, the glacial dam failed and the lake drained catastrophically. Water drained from the lake at a rate of about 10^5 m^3/s, and the water level in the lake dropped 25 m in one day. The circumstances of Lake Wisconsin's drainage were very similar, so it seems likely that it also drained catastrophically. The volume of water that drained from Lake Wisconsin was several times greater than the

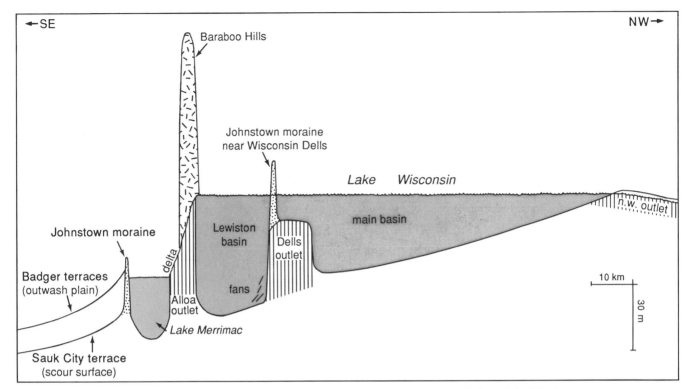

Figure 38. Profile of Lake Wisconsin just as the Lewiston basin started to drain to Lake Merrimac. Elevations have been adjusted to remove the effect of later crustal rebound. The vertically ruled areas are outlets.

flood from Russell Fiord, and for this reason the Lake Wisconsin flood probably lasted a few days.

One of the best-known pre-modern examples of a catastrophic flood from a glacial lake occurred in Washington, Idaho, and Montana during the Wisconsin Glaciation (Baker and Nummedal, 1978; Baker and Bunker, 1985). The glacial dam of Lake Missoula failed, causing the Spokane Floods. The lake held a much greater volume of water than Lake Wisconsin, and the drop in water level was much greater; as a result the flood was much larger. The most obvious results of this flood were the network of huge channels cut in basalt in southeastern Washington and associated bedforms and bedload deposits with boulders several meters in diameter.

Is there any evidence that Lake Wisconsin flooded catastrophically? The most likely places for such evidence are at the Alloa outlet, where the primary flood would have occurred, and at the Dells outlet, where the main basin would have flooded into the Lewiston basin.

The Alloa flood

The Alloa delta, where the Alloa outlet emptied into Lake Merrimac, has been described by J Harlen Bretz (1950), who is well known for his 1920s hypothesis of a catastrophic Spokane

Flood. Bretz observed the sediment of the Alloa delta in a pit (Fig. 39) that exposed "foresets of extraordinary open-work coarse gravel" that dip southward and are 12 m or more high. He noted that the gravel contains boulders as large as 1.5 m in diameter, and he stated that the only more bouldery delta he had ever seen was at the head of a fiord in Greenland. The pit is still in operation; a working face a few hundred meters long exposes 7 m of foreset beds containing abundant boulders of Baraboo quartzite as well as Precambrian and Paleozoic lithologies glacially transported from more distant sources.

Bretz referred to the Alloa delta as a "torrential delta," and he recognized that it was the result of the drainage of Lake Wisconsin into Lake Merrimac. However, he said (p. 135), with-

Figure 39. Topographic map of the Alloa outlet (arrows indicate flow direction). Heavy dashed line in the north is the shoreline of Lake Wisconsin during the Elderon Phase; in the south, Lake Merrimac. The heavy solid line with tick marks is the margin of the Green Bay Lobe. The high area in the northwest is the Baraboo quartzite of the Baraboo Hills. The area north of Lake Merrimac is the Alloa delta. The Wisconsin River is in the southeast corner. The west half is from the U.S. Geological Survey's Durwards Glen Quadrangle (7.5 minute series; 1978; 20-ft contour interval) and the east half is from the Poynette Quadrangle (7.5 minute series; 1984; 10-ft contour interval). Location shown in Figure 11 (T.11 and 12N.,R.8 and 9E.).

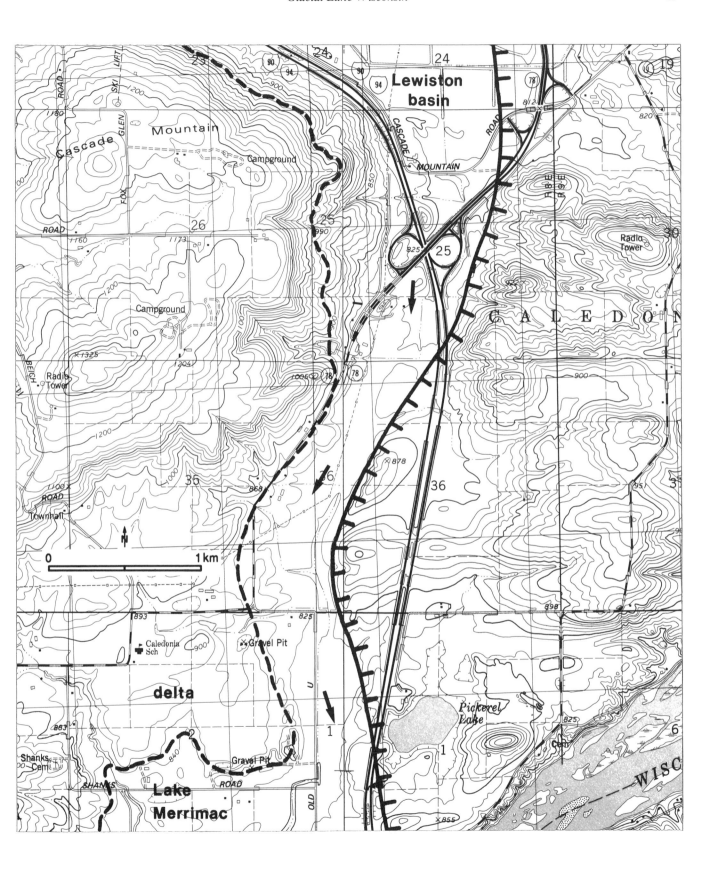

out giving evidence, that "no debacle occurred during this failure of the ice barrier at the east end of the [Baraboo] Ranges."

Alden (1918, p. 288), however, seemed to think there was an Alloa debacle; he noted that "the discharge of such a volume of water must have been an event of considerable moment." Curiously, Alden later became a vigorous critic of Bretz's Spokane Flood hypothesis (Baker and Nummedal, 1978, p. 8–9).

Water began to flow through the Alloa outlet when the lake level was about 295 m; at that time, the west bank was nearly unerodible Baraboo quartzite, and the east bank was the easily eroded glacier. The water quickly downcut through the ice as the lake drained until it stabilized at a more normal discharge, with the lake level probably somewhat above the level of the present-day saddle between the 820-ft and 830-ft (250-m and 253-m) contours at point **a** in Figure 9. After the lake had dropped below about 275 m, the east bank of the outlet channel was Cambrian sandstone. During at least the early part of this drainage event, the water flowing from the Alloa outlet into Lake Merrimac formed the Alloa delta at an elevation of about 264 m, shown in the lower left quarter of Figure 39.

The large boulders in the delta can probably be considered to be good evidence for the Alloa flood. The 1.5-m boulders observed by Bretz in the Alloa pit were deposited 1.5 km downstream from the Alloa channel; comparable sized boulders are found 7 to 20 km downstream from constrictions in the path of the much larger Spokane Flood (Baker and Nummedal, 1978, Table 4.23). The gravel of the Alloa delta is comparable in size to gravel deposited by catastrophic floods from large glacial lakes in North Dakota and Saskatchewan (cobble gravel with 1-m boulders, rarely 3-m boulders; Kehew and Lord, 1987, p. 103), northwestern Ontario (boulders commonly more than 0.5 m in diameter, occasionally more than 3 m; Teller and Thorliefson, 1983, p. 278–279), and northern Wisconsin (1.5-m boulders; Clayton, 1984, p. 20).

Large channels are a characteristic feature of the Spokane Flood and of the midcontinental glacial-lake floods. However, such channels are not a conspicuous feature of the Alloa flood, probably because the quartzite of the Baraboo Hills is nearly unerodible. The Alloa outlet channel was about 1 km wide (Fig. 39), but most of the east bank of the channel is now missing because it was cut in ice. The Alloa delta is small compared to those formed during other glacial-lake floods, but there was little material available to form a delta because of the resistance to erosion of the quartzite in the Alloa channel. In contrast, channels are the conspicuous feature today in the area of the Dells flood.

The Dells flood

We think it likely that an Alloa flood did occur, and it seems likely that the water level in the Lewiston basin dropped at least 30 m in a few days (Fig. 38). If so, the direction of flow in the Dells outlet quickly reversed as the water in the Hulburt basin, the Dell Creek basin, and the main basin began to flood into the emptying Lewiston basin (Figs. 4 and 11). The Lewiston basin

and Hulburt basin are separated from each other by the Johnstown moraine, which is a few hundred meters wide in this area—small enough to have been quickly washed away. After the water level in the main basin dropped about 10 m, most of the Pleistocene sediment in the Dells area had been washed away, leaving soft sandstone of the Mt. Simon Formation for a distance of 9 km upstream from the moraine. Here the Dells flood or its successor, the Wisconsin River, has cut a series of sandstone gorges called the Wisconsin Dells, which is also the name of the resort city 3 km upstream from the moraine. The relationship between the moraine, the sandstone gorges, and the basins is shown in Figure 38.

The term "dells" (or "dalles") has generally been used in Wisconsin for a river-cut rock gorge, and many of them have been cut by water from glacial lakes. The Wisconsin Dells consist of a complex network of gorges about 10 km long. The central gorge, occupied today by the Wisconsin River, is typically about 0.2 km wide, but it is 15 m wide at the Narrows; the gorge is about 40 m deep in many places (Fig. 40). This gorge is most conveniently viewed from a boat. Side gorges such as Witches Gulch and Coldwater Canyon are tens of meters deep but narrow to a width of 1 m in places. They are also accessible by boat. Many of the associated gorges lack modern-day streams, and many of them cross local drainage divides. A typical example of a nearly dry dell can be seen in Rocky Arbor State Park; this gorge is 0.2 km wide, 20 to 30 m deep, and 2 km long (Fig. 40). At its northeast end it joins the Wisconsin River gorge, and at its southwest end it joins the Hulburt Creek gorge.

Martin (1916, p. 329) suggested that the gorges on the east side of the Wisconsin River, such as Coldwater Canyon (Fig. 40), were cut by meltwater rivers when the glacier stood at the Johnstown moraine to the east. This was impossible, however, because whenever meltwater flowed west toward this area it was submerged in Lake Wisconsin. Martin (p. 330–331) thought that other gorges were gradually cut by postglacial rivers. Those with modern rivers in them have to some degree been modified by those rivers. Those without streams and those that cross local drainage divides, however, must have been cut by pre-modern rivers, and therefore it seems likely that those with streams today were also at least initiated by pre-modern rivers. Because the Dells occur where flood gorges are expected, it is likely that they were in fact cut by a catastrophic flood, probably at least down to about 30 m below the predrainage lake level (Fig. 38). Further deepening of the Wisconsin River gorge may have taken a much longer time.

Figure 40. Topographic map of part of the Wisconsin Dells. The heavy dashed line is the shoreline during the Elderon Phase. Arrows indicate direction of water movement through the sandstone gorges at the time they were cut. U.S. Geological Survey Wisconsin Dells North Quadrangle (7.5 minute series; 10-ft contour interval; 1975). Location of Dells outlet shown in Figure 11 (T.13 and 14N.,R.5E., on the northwest edge of the city of Wisconsin Dells).

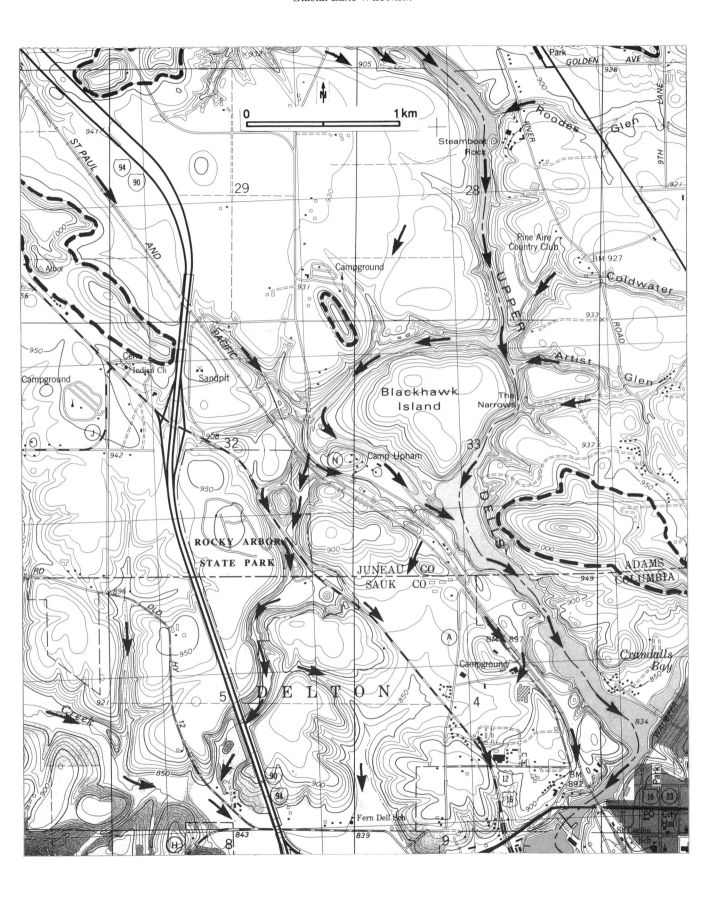

The Dells gorges are typically only roughly a tenth as large as those cut by the much larger Spokane Flood and midcontinent glacial-lake floods, but they form a similar anastomosing network. In addition, a zone several kilometers wide upstream from the moraine has been scoured free of lake sediment, exposing sandstone at the surface throughout the Dells area. The proposed Dells flood seems the only likely explanation.

Coarse flood sediment has not been observed in the Dells area, perhaps because the bottoms of the gorges are filled with younger sediment. It is likely that the soft sandstone quickly disintegrated to sand, and the main source of coarse sediment was the Johnstown moraine. Fans of sediment downstream from the moraine (Fig. 38) are largely sand and gravel with pebbles and cobbles derived from the moraine.

The flood down the Wisconsin River

If these interpretations are correct, the initial flood down the Wisconsin River consisted of a catastrophic discharge from the Lewiston basin as the water level dropped 30 m within a few days. This initial flood in part coincided with a somewhat more drawn out flood as the Johnstown moraine was entrenched and as the sandstone gorges were cut at the Dells. A somewhat similar sequence of events may have occurred several times near the end of the Wisconsin Glaciation. A flood must have occurred each time the ice margin wasted back past the east end of the Baraboo Hills. If the ice margin advanced onto the east end of the Baraboo Hills again, the basin refilled. Several Elderon moraines occur northeast of Lake Wisconsin, indicating that the Green Bay Lobe may have fluctuated when it was at the east end of the Baraboo Hills about the time the lake drained.

The intensity of the initial flood was probably diminished by its passage through the constrictions in the basin of Lake Merrimac (Fig. 11), but it was still vigorous enough to shift the outlet of Lake Merrimac from the Badger outlet to the more direct Sauk City outlet (Fig. 11). The water in Lake Merrimac dropped about 20 m as the discharging water cut down through the Johnstown moraine and outwash plain to the level of the surfaces between elevations of 230 m and 240 m at Sauk City (Figs. 32 and 38).

The Sauk City surfaces are underlain by slightly gravelly sand that contains isolated boulders of Baraboo quartzite, some with a long axis up to 1 m. Farther downstream, the presence of quartzite boulders indicates that flood water reached an elevation of about 225 m (20 m above present river level) about halfway between the Alloa outlet and the junction of the Wisconsin and Mississippi Rivers (Knox and Attig, 1988). These boulders were probably rafted by icebergs dislodged from the Alloa outlet area during the flood. Other evidence of flooding through the lower Wisconsin valley is the scouring of loess from the eastern part of the Bridgeport terrace, an eastward sloping pre-Wisconsin outwash surface (Knox and Attig, 1988). Late Wisconsin loess has been stripped from the surface of the Bridgeport terrace where it is below the highest level of the flood from Lake Wisconsin.

The impact of the Lake Wisconsin floods beyond the junc-

tion of the Wisconsin and Mississippi Rivers is unknown. During the last part of the Wisconsin Glaciation the Mississippi valley was subject to floods from Lake Agassiz as well as from ice-marginal lakes in the western part of the Lake Superior basin (Flock, 1983). The details of the flood history of the upper Mississippi valley are obscure, and therefore it is impossible at this time to distinguish the effects of the Lake Wisconsin floods.

PERMAFROST

Permafrost is thought to have existed in central Wisconsin from about 25,000 years ago until about 13,000 years ago (Attig and Clayton, 1986; in preparation). The existence of permafrost around Lake Wisconsin had a major influence on the formation and preservation of shoreline features and on the transport of sediment from the glacier to the lake. We here briefly review the evidence for permafrost near Lake Wisconsin and its effect on the deposits and landforms.

The most widespread evidence of permafrost around Lake Wisconsin is ice-wedge polygons. They are clearly visible on 1:20,000 aerial photographs at several dozen sites, which are indicated in Figure 33. Most occur on outwash and offshore sand on the east side of the main basin in Portage, Adams, and Juneau Counties (illustrated by Clayton, 1986, 1987, 1989b). Individual polygons are typically 10 to 100 m in diameter. They have no topographic expression but consist of light or dark bands a few meters wide that generally intersect in Y junctions, forming distinct polygons. The presence of wedge-shaped forms beneath the margins of the polygons has been confirmed at several sites using ground-penetrating radar (Attig and others, 1987). The presence of ice-wedge polygons on the lake plain indicates that permafrost existed until after Lake Wisconsin drained.

Ice-wedge casts have been seen in outcrop in a few places in the area. The casts are typically several meters long and a meter or less wide. The casts are formed in offshore sand or meltwater-stream sand that is overlain by wind-blown sand. Although the wedges are typically only a meter or so wide, the collapse trench at the top of the wedge is typically several meters wide. The trenches are filled with wind-blown sand, and as a result they have no topographic expression. The wind-blown sand is finer than the offshore or meltwater-stream sand. This difference in grain size causes differences in moisture-holding ability. As a result, the polygonal patterns of the ice-wedge casts show up on aerial photographs because of differences in vegetation or soil moisture.

Other possible evidence of permafrost includes gullies extending back into the outwash plain north of Wisconsin Dells (Fig. 41). The gullies are now inactive. No streams exist in the headward parts of the gullies, and no stream erosion is now taking place. The outwash into which the gullies are cut is highly permeable sand, and as a result, most precipitation infiltrates and little slope-wash erosion takes place. The gullies were probably cut when the water table was higher, perhaps as a result of the presence of permafrost.

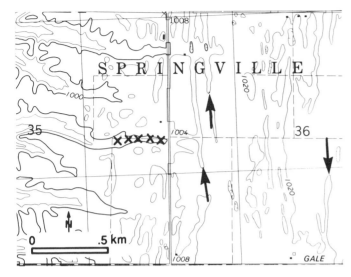

Figure 41. Topographic map of gullies cut into delta on southeast side of main basin of Lake Wisconsin, in the south-central part of the area shown in Figure 21 (T.15N.,R.6E.). Arrows indicate examples of contours that outline shore-ice collapse trenches. The Xs indicate places where collapse trenches shown on aerial photographs cross through the bottoms of gullies. U.S. Geological Survey Big Spring Quadrangle (7.5 minute series; 10-ft contour interval; 1975).

Clayton and Attig (1987a) discussed evidence that the gullies were cut before the last ground ice melted. Shore-ice collapse trenches (discussed earlier) occur between the gullies (Fig. 41). They formed where ice had been buried in outwash along the shore of Lake Wisconsin, the actual formation occurring when the buried shore ice melted, causing the overlying outwash to collapse. Many of these trenches can be traced across the outwash plain, down the sides of the gullies, and across their bottoms, indicating that the ice melted after the gullies were cut. The outwash was deposited and the ice was buried before the end of the Johnstown Phase of glaciation, and the gullies were cut after the lake drained at the end of the Elderon Phase of glaciation—a period of at least a few hundred years. The shore ice could persist this long only if there was permafrost, and the melting of the shore ice occurred when the permafrost melted. Therefore, Lake Wisconsin drained and the gullies were cut before permafrost melted. The gullies have been inactive since then.

Attig and others (1989b) argue that the presence of tunnel channels formed under the glacier also suggests the presence of permafrost. The channels are an order of magnitude larger than typical eskers in the area and they are closely spaced, indicating that each channel may have been cut by an extraordinary discharge of meltwater for a short period of time. In Wisconsin, tunnel channels formed in a zone 5 to 20 km wide where the margin of the glacier was apparently frozen to its bed. The tunnel channels east of Lake Wisconsin are about 10 km long, indicating a frozen zone about that wide. The tunnel channels were cut when meltwater from the thawing-bed part of the glacier broke through the frozen-bed zone along the margin. A frozen bed along the margin of the glacier is consistent with evidence of permafrost beyond the ice margin. The outwash deposited in the east side of the main basin came largely from tunnel channels

(Fig. 37), as did the offshore sand in the eastern half of the main basin. In a previous section we have suggested that sand was carried far out into the basin because of the high velocities associated with underflow currents resulting from tunnel-channel outbursts.

Other features that may be related to permafrost are the extensive talus in Devils Lake gorge and fossil rock glaciers in the Baraboo Hills. The talus below the quartzite cliffs in Devils Lake gorge is buried beneath the moraine at the south end of the gorge and is now inactive. Smith (1949) argued that the talus is the result of a tundra climate during the last glaciation. Boulder streams in the Baraboo Hills (Attig and others, 1989c; Smith, 1949) have been interpreted to be rock glaciers, also a permafrost feature.

In summary, continuous permafrost occurred around Lake Wisconsin during most of its existence and for some time after it drained, until about 13,000 years ago. This permafrost had a considerable effect on the lake's deposits and landforms. It was responsible for the tunnel-channel floods that transported sand far out into the eastern part of the main basin, and it was in part responsible for the preservation of the shore ice that was under the collapse trenches. In addition, it was probably responsible for the poor preservation of beaches and other lake features. Small-scale glacial landforms in the parts of Wisconsin glaciated before about 13,000 BP are very poorly preserved, whereas those formed after that time are well preserved. The coincidence of this date with the time of the disappearance of permafrost indicates that the permafrost was the probable cause of the greater erosion on the earlier glacial landforms. Solifluction, slope wash, and other hillslope processes that are enhanced by permafrost were probably the main factors in the poor preservation of Lake Wisconsin beach ridges and terraces.

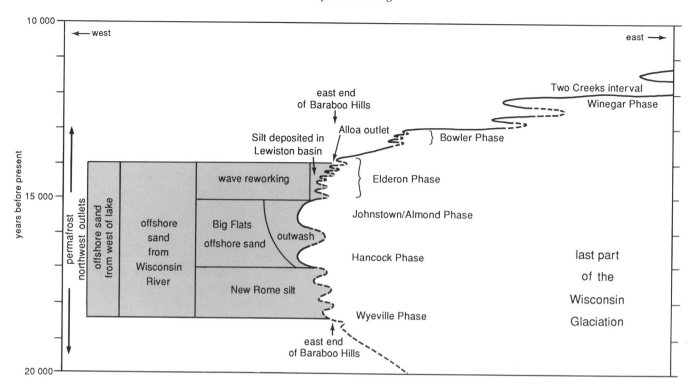

Figure 42. Time-distance diagram showing chronology of Lake Wisconsin events during the last part of the Wisconsin Glaciation. The vertical axis is time, and the horizontal axis is distance. The gray area represents Lake Wisconsin. The sinuous line is the margin of the ice sheet.

CHRONOLOGY

We have reviewed the outlets, shorelines, and offshore sediment of Lake Wisconsin and have made comments on the events that were responsible for their formation. Here we discuss the timing of the events (Fig. 42). Few radiocarbon dates are available from the region, and therefore the chronology of Lake Wisconsin can be established only by correlation with better dated events in surrounding regions.

Most of the features discussed in this memoir are the result of events related to the last glaciation in the region, which we have referred to as "the last part of the Wisconsin Glaciation." The chronology of these glacial events has been reviewed by Mickelson and others (1983), Attig and others (1985), and Eschman and Mickelson (1986). The glacier expanded into central Wisconsin at least six times prior to the last part of the Wisconsin Glaciation (during the Stetsonville, Milan, Marshfield, Nasonville, Arnott, and Hamburg phases); these events have been documented in Portage County (Clayton, 1986), Wood County (Clayton, 1989a), and Marathon County (Attig and Muldoon, 1989), just north of Lake Wisconsin. Other earlier and intervening glacial phases may also have occurred.

It is unknown if the glacier reached the east end of the Baraboo Hills during these early phases, but it probably did during at least the Arnott Phase. The Arnott moraine in Portage County, just northeast of the main basin of Lake Wisconsin, is parallel to and just west of the outermost moraine formed during the last part of the Wisconsin Glaciation. South of Portage County, it is either under or east of the Johnstown moraine (Fig. 4). It is probably not very far east of the Johnstown moraine, however, and it seems likely that the previously discussed submerged ridge between the Lewiston basin and the main basin (at the time the New Rome silt was being deposited) was the Arnott moraine, with its outwash plain. If so, the Arnott glacier reached the Baraboo Hills. If the Devils Lake gorge had been clogged before the Wyeville Phase, as suggested above, some pre-Wyeville glacier, perhaps during the Arnott Phase, must have moved as far west as Devils Nose (southeast of Devils Lake; Fig. 19), almost as far as during the Johnstown Phase. Therefore, it seems likely that sometime before the last part of the Wisconsin Glaciation, probably during the Arnott Phase, Lake Wisconsin rose to the level of the northwest outlet, formed a set of shorelines much like the Wyeville, Johnstown, and Elderon, and deposited a bed of silt much like the New Rome bed as well as a large amount of offshore sand. Clayton (1986, p. 6) has discussed the reasons for thinking the Arnott Phase occurred before the late part of the Wisconsin Glaciation and probably before the early part as well. During this or a similar pre-Wyeville event, the pre-Wyeville shoreline discussed in an earlier section formed, and the offshore sediment below the New Rome silt bed was deposited.

This pre-Wyeville event was followed by at least one interglacial interval if the pre-Wyeville event occurred before the early part of the Wisconsin Glaciation as suggested above. No evidence is known that the glacier reached this area during the early part of the Wisconsin Glaciation, and it seems unlikely that Lake Wisconsin existed then.

The beginning of the last part of the Wisconsin Glaciation in this region is commonly placed around 25,000 or 20,000 BP. Several radiocarbon dates from wood under till or meltwater sediment in Wisconsin are around 30,000 BP; the latest is 26,060 ± 800 BP (W-2022; Attig and others, 1985) from spruce wood under 60 m of meltwater-stream sediment near Menominee, Wisconsin. Eschman and Mickelson (1986, Chart 1) and Johnson (1986, Chart 1), in their summaries of the chronology of the Green Bay and Lake Michigan Lobes, estimate the last major expansion of the glacier into southeastern Wisconsin and northwestern Illinois to have begun roughly 23,000 BP (Fig. 42). Lake Wisconsin came into existence well after the beginning of this expansion, and therefore a reasonable estimate for the date of the Wyeville Phase is perhaps around 19,000 or 18,000 BP.

The Johnstown Phase has never been precisely dated. Radiocarbon dates from wood in postglacial sediment in southeastern Wisconsin indicate that it occurred before 12,800 ± 200 (WIS-48) and 13,120 ± 130 BP (WIS-431; Bender and others, 1965 and 1971). Clayton and Moran (1982, Fig. 1), on the basis of indefinite regional correlations, suggested it occurred about 15,000 BP. Mickelson and others (1983, p. 23) suggested that the Green Bay Lobe remained near its maximum position until about 13,000 BP, based on radiocarbon dates from Devils Lake, but these dates more likely mark the end of tundra conditions. The Johnstown moraine probably correlates with the West Chicago moraine of the Lake Michigan Lobe, which is composed of till of the Haeger Member (Mickelson and others, 1983, p. 23). Johnson (1986, chart 1) suggested that the Haeger till was deposited around 16,500 or 16,000 BP, but no wood dates are available from this material. We therefore suggest that the Johnstown Phase occurred around 16,000 or 15,000 BP.

The New Rome silt was interpreted in a previous section to have been deposited, at least in part, from the time of the Wyeville Phase to just before the Johnstown Phase, or from roughly 19,000 to 18,000 BP to roughly 17,000 BP. At least the upper and eastern part of the New Rome was deposited closer to the time of the Johnstown Phase than to the time of the Wyeville Phase, because the New Rome bed at the east edge of the basin is above the level of the Wyeville shoreline. Rhythmically bedded, probably varved, silt was observed in a borrow pit at UTM coordinates YU3776-5323, 2 km east of Mauston, in Juneau County. The varves are 2 to 13 mm thick, averaging about 5 mm, and the exposed varve sequence is 2 m thick, with about 400 varves. This is overlain by 1 m of presently unbedded (bioturbated) silt and underlain by about 1 m of unexposed silt; extrapolating, with the assumption of uniform sedimentation, gives about 800 years of deposition.

The Elderon Phase has never been directly dated, but the Elderon moraines have been correlated with material in other areas that has been assigned ages. In Portage County, just northeast of the main basin of Lake Wisconsin, Clayton (1986, p. 18) suggested that the Elderon Phase occurred around 14,000 or 13,000 BP. Attig and others (1985, Fig. 6) correlated the Elderon moraines with moraines in northern Wisconsin (Clayton, 1984, Figs. 23, 24, and 26) and Minnesota that Clayton and Moran (1982, Fig. 1) suggested formed around 14,000 to 12,500 BP. In central Wisconsin, the Elderon Phase is known to have occurred largely (or entirely) before about 13,000 BP, when the last permafrost melted (Attig and Clayton, 1986), because ice-wedge polygons formed on the plain of Lake Wisconsin after it drained. To the southeast, the Elderon moraines correlate with the Lake Mills moraines (Alden, 1918). Wood in postglacial sediment on Lake Mills till has been dated 13,120 ± 130 BP (WIS-431; Bender and others, 1971). Correlation southeastward to the Lake Michigan Lobe is unclear, but the Lake Mills moraines may correlate with the younger Valparaiso moraines of northeastern Illinois (Alden, 1918), which Johnson (1986, chart 1, p. 21) suggested were formed about 15,500 BP, based on radiocarbon dates from postglacial peat and bone (both are materials that are commonly contaminated with older material) dated 15,240 ± 120 (ISGS-465) and 13,130 ± 350 BP (ISGS-485). We therefore suggest that the last part of the Elderon Phase, when Lake Wisconsin drained for the last time, occurred roughly 14,000 BP (Fig. 42).

After Lake Wisconsin drained, the Wisconsin River flowed across the main basin, downcut through the lake sediment, and stabilized or aggraded slightly to form the Love terrace 2 to 5 m below the level of the lake plain (Clayton, 1986, 1987, 1989a, 1989b; Attig and Muldoon, 1989). Through Portage and Wood Counties and the northern parts of Adams and Juneau Counties, the Love terrace is 10 to 20 m above the modern floodplain of the Wisconsin River, but southward the terrace becomes closer to the floodplain until they merge near the north end of the Wisconsin Dells. In contrast to lower terraces, the Love terrace has braided channel scars rather than meandering channel scars, suggesting that the sediment was deposited by glacial meltwater. Attig and Muldoon (1989) suggest that this happened during the Winegar Phase of the Ontonagon Lobe (an extension of the Superior Lobe), when glacial meltwater flowed down the Wisconsin River for the last time. The Winegar Phase occurred just before the Two Creeks interval (12,200 to 11,500 BP), perhaps around 13,000 or 12,500 BP (Attig and others, 1985). The Love terrace, like the Winegar surfaces, lacks evidence of permafrost and was formed just after it finally melted.

GREAT LAKES CRUSTAL REBOUND

Larsen (1987) has outlined the history of the hinge-line model for crustal rebound in the Great Lakes area at the end of the Wisconsin Glaciation. The shorelines formed in the proglacial Great Lakes at the end of the Wisconsin Glaciation have long been known to be tilted. The oldest and steepest shorelines were generally thought to be tilted southwestward as far as a "hinge line," southwest of which no tilting occurred after about 13,000 BP. In Lake Michigan, the so-called hinge line was thought to be near the middle of the lake.

This hinge-line concept has recently been challenged (Larsen, 1987), partly because of the observation that crustal rebound is continuing today throughout the Great Lakes area; northern Lake Superior is now being uplifted 0.5 m/century compared to southern Lake Michigan. The hinge line has been reinterpreted to be the crossing line of older, steeper water planes (such as the Algonquin) with younger, less steep water planes (such as the Nipissing), as shown in Figure 24e.

Guetter and others (1987) have pointed out that the tilted shorelines of Lake Wisconsin provide a test of the hinge-line model. Lake Wisconsin is southwest of the supposed Great Lakes hinge line, but considerable rebound occurred here after the Elderon shoreline formed, after about 14,000 BP. It seems unlikely that crustal rebound would cease sometime after the Elderon shoreline formed but before the first shorelines formed in the southern end of Lake Michigan around 13,000 BP, to be resumed again in historic time.

CONCLUSION

The history of proglacial Lake Wisconsin has been known in broad outline for 70 years. Partly as the result of inadequate topographic maps, however, the lake received little detailed study before 1982. We have reported on our recent findings, and we have related these to our modern understanding of the late Pleistocene history of the western Great Lakes region. We have placed considerable emphasis on the construction of shoreline profiles. Although the evidence for shorelines is generally obscure, we have some confidence in our reconstructions because the required crustal tilt is similar to that independently predicted on geophysical grounds.

Little is known about the earlier versions of the lake, before the last glaciation, just as little is known about earlier glaciations and the earlier geomorphic history of the region. It seems most likely that future information on the early lakes will be found in deeply buried offshore deposits, which to date have scarcely been sampled. An improvement in our understanding of the more recent history of the lake will in part depend on more radiometric dates from lake deposits and from associated glacial and fluvial deposits. More detailed sedimentological studies are needed to confirm the existence of shore deposits and to relate them more closely to water levels, and sedimentological studies of offshore sand exposed in the wave-cut bluffs of reservoirs along the Wisconsin River may prove enlightening. The continued development of our understanding of the erosional history of the region, the depositional history in the lower Wisconsin valley, and the movement of the Earth's crust will undoubtedly also greatly improve our understanding of the lake history.

ACKNOWLEDGMENTS

David M. Mickelson discussed various aspects of glacial Lake Wisconsin with us and made helpful comments on an early version of this report. Robert W. Baker and William N. Mode reviewed the manuscript and made many useful suggestions. Brenda Haskins-Grahn prepared the illustrations.

A Photo Essay of
Glacial Lake Wisconsin Area

Photos by
Lee Clayton and John W. Attig
unless otherwise credited

Photos A and B (this and facing page). General area of the South Bluff outlet, one of the possible northwestern outlets of Lake Wisconsin. This flat area of bog and low sand dunes, which is several kilometres wide, is today the lowest part of the divide between the Wisconsin and Black River valleys. No channel form is visible here today, probably because it has been destroyed by eolian erosion or filled with modern fluvial, eolian, and swamp sediment. Photograph A was taken from near the west edge of the map in Figure 8 (NW¼Sec.10,T.21N.,R.2E.); view to west-southwest. Hills in the distance consist of Cambrian sandstone. Photograph B was taken from the road near the south edge of Figure 8; view to south.

Photo C. The North Bluff outlet, one of the northwestern outlets of Lake Wisconsin. View to the north at the fence marking the south boundary of the Sandhill State Wildlife area (southwest part of the map in Fig. 9). The channel, which has been nearly filled with modern sediment, is marked by a strip of bog bordered by forested sand dunes.

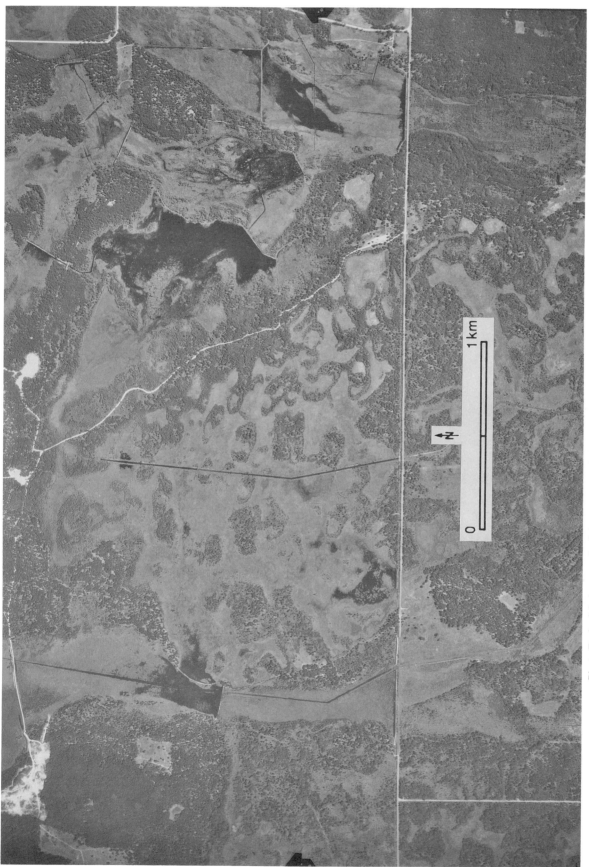

Photo D. Aerial photograph of the area around the North Bluff outlet and west Babcock outlet of Lake Wisconsin; the outlets can be located by comparing with the topographic map shown in Figure 9. The black areas are open water. The speckled dark gray areas are forested sand dunes. The uniform light gray areas are bog. The white areas are roads, gravel pits, and rock quarries; the gravel pit in the northwest corner is on the northwest side of North Bluff, in a pre-Wyeville beach. (U.S. Department of Agriculture, Agricultural Stabilization and Conservation Service photograph BIL–6AA–136, taken in 1960.)

Photo E. Aerial photograph of cranberry bogs (the uniformly rectangular fields) at the north end of the plain of Lake Wisconsin, 15 km southwest of the city of Wisconsin Rapids. This is one of the major cranberry-producing regions in the nation. The water table is near the surface because this is a low region between the offshore-sediment fan derived from the Yellow and Hemlock Rivers (to the west) and that derived from the Wisconsin River (to the east). The areas of open water (black) contain floating mats of peat. The larger mats still retain their original shape, with angular edges where the peat was cut by ditches. Like pieces of a jig-saw puzzle, these mats could be fitted back into their original position. The smaller peat mats are rounded because they have floated around enough to abraid their corners. Highway 54 runs east-west through the middle of the area. (U.S. Department of Agriculture, Agricultural Stabilization and Conservation Service photograph BIL–6AA–28, taken in 1960.)

Photo F. A rare exposure of Lake Wisconsin beach sediment. The gravel was deposited during the Johnstown Phase on the southeast side of an island in the northern end of Lake Wisconsin (gravel pit in the southeast corner of Sec.28,T.22N.,R.4E.).

Photo G. Typical view of the flat plain of Lake Wisconsin, looking north along Highway 80, near the community of Sprague, in northern Juneau County. Much of the Lake Wisconsin plain is forested offshore sand with the water table just below the surface.

Photos H and I. Sand dunes on the Lake Wisconsin plain, in northwestern Adams County (Sec.13,T.19N.,R.5E.). The parabolic dunes in this area are as much as 20 m high, formed by winds from the west-northwest, probably during the dry period in middle Holocene time; here they are covered with pine plantations, with newly planted pines in the foreground. Over most of the rest of the lake plain, dunes are no more than a few meters high.

Photo J. Shore stacks at Rabbit Rock, which rises above the offshore plain in the eastern part of the main basin of Lake Wisconsin. The stacks are within a wayside park next to Highway 13, 13 km north of the village of Friendship. The rock is Cambrian sandstone.

Photo K. Shore cliffs on the sides of Roch a Cri, an outlier of Cambrian sandstone rising above the offshore plain in the eastern part of the main basin of Lake Wisconsin, in Roch a Cri State Park, 3 km north of the village of Friendship.

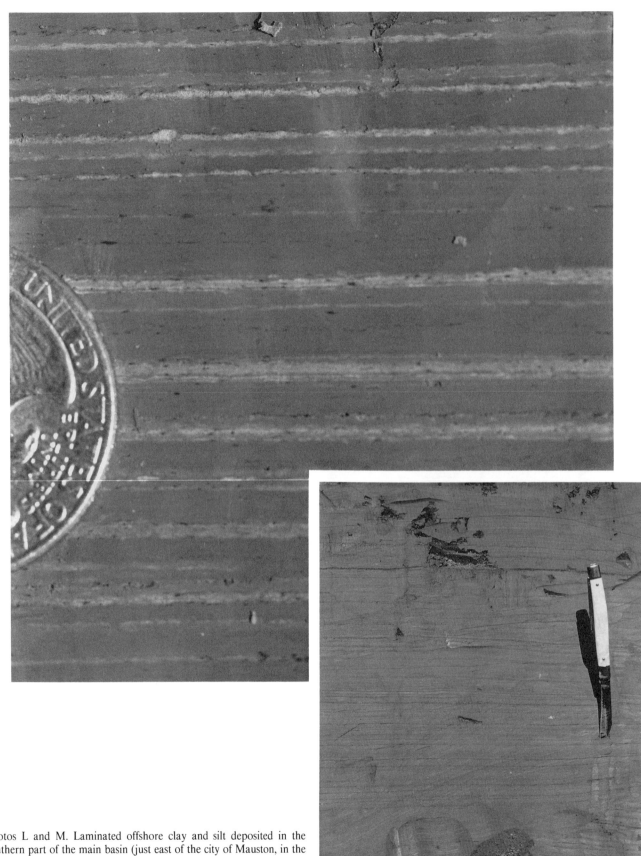

Photos L and M. Laminated offshore clay and silt deposited in the southern part of the main basin (just east of the city of Mauston, in the SW¼SW¼NE¼Sec.8,T.15N.,R.4E.).

Photo N. The Wonewoc escarpment, forming the southwest side of the main basin of Lake Wisconsin (the location of the escarpment is shown in Fig. 4). The escarpment is capped with hard sandstone of the Ironton Member, at the top of the Wonewoc Formation. The foreground is underlain by offshore sand. Photograph taken looking west from the SE¼Sec.13,T.15N.,R.3E., 1 km south of the city of Mauston.

Photo O. Shore-ice collapse trenches paralleling the southeast shore of the main basin of Lake Wisconsin. They formed where stranded lake ice was buried by sand deposited by meltwater rivers flowing from the Green Bay Lobe, which was 2 km to the east. The distribution of the trenches is shown in Figure 21. The view here is to the west, perpendicular to the trenches, from Highway B (middle of the south edge of Fig. 22).

Photo P. Witches Gulch, one of the northern-most sandstone gorges of the Wisconsin Dells area. Witches Gulch is 1 km long, tens of meters deep, and as narrow as 1 m. Scale here is indicated by the boardwalk in the lower-left part of the photograph. This gorge and similar gorges in the Dells area were at least in part cut by the catastrophic flood when Lake Wisconsin suddenly drained as the Green Bay Lobe melted back from the east end of the Baraboo Hills. The photograph was taken by Henry Hamilton Bennett in the 1880s (photograph 1049, reproduced with permission of the H. H. Bennett Studio, Inc.).

Photo Q. Berrys Landing, between Witches Gulch and The Narrows in the Upper Dells, north of the city of Wisconsin Dells. The Wisconsin River gorge was at least in part cut into the Cambrian sandstone by the catastrophic flood when Lake Wisconsin drained. The photograph was taken by Henry Hamilton Bennett in the 1880s, before the Dells dam was constructed, raising the water level here (photograph 279, reproduced with permission of the H. H. Bennett Studio, Inc.).

Photo R. The Narrows in the Upper Dells; the Wisconsin River gorge here is only about 15 m wide (the locality is labeled in Fig. 40). The photograph was taken by Henry Hamilton Bennett in the 1880s, before the Dells dam was constructed, raising the water level here (photograph 1018, reproduced with permission of the H. H. Bennett Studio, Inc.).

Photo S. The Jaws of the Upper Dells, 1.7 km north of the present dam at the city of Wisconsin Dells (Fig. 40). Boat tours of the gorge attract numerous tourists. The gorges in the Wisconsin Dells area are walled with sandstone of the Elk Mound Group (Cambrian). The photograph was taken by Henry Hamilton Bennett in the 1880s (photograph 2018, reproduced with permission of the H. H. Bennett Studio, Inc.).

Photo T. The Lower Dells of the Wisconsin River, south of the city of Wisconsin Dells. The sandstone gorges in the Dells were at least in part cut by the catastrophic flood when Lake Wisconsin drained. The photograph was taken by Henry Hamilton Bennett in the 1880s (photograph 109 reproduced with permission of the H. H. Bennett Studio, Inc.).

Photo U. Mirror Lake in the Dell Creek gorge, which was cut when water drained from the Dell Creek basin to the Hulburt basin of Lake Wisconsin. The photograph was taken looking southwest from the bridge by the Mirror Lake dam, shown in the upper-right part of the map in Figure 12.

Photo V. Aerial stereogram of the Dell Creek gorge, which was cut when water drained from the Dell Creek basin to the Hulburt basin of Lake Wisconsin; compare with the topographic map in Figure 12. The divided highway (Interstate 90-94), where it crosses the gorge, runs along the former drainage divide that separated the two basins before the gorge was cut. Much of the area is southwest of Interstate 90-94 in Mirror Lake State Park. (U.S. Department of Agriculture, Agricultural Stabilization and Conservation Service photographs WR–2JI–155, 156, and 157, taken in 1968.)

Photo W. Aerial stereogram of the Upper Narrows outlet of the Reedsburg basin and the Narrows Creek outlet of the Loganville basin of Lake Wisconsin; compare with the topographic map in Figure 15. These two outlets cut through the North Range of the Baraboo Hills, which are cored with quartzite of the Baraboo Formation (Precambrian). The village of Rock Springs is on the south end of the Upper Narrows of the Baraboo River. (U.S. Department of Agriculture, Agricultural Stabilization and Conservation Service photographs WR–2JJ–269, 270, and 271, taken in 1968.)

Photo X. The Lower Narrows outlet of the east Baraboo basin of Lake Wisconsin. The Lower Narrows of the Baraboo River cut through the North Range of the Baraboo Hills, which are composed of quartzite of the Baraboo Formation (Precambrian). View to the north-northeast from the South Range, looking across the east Baraboo basin, through the Lower Narrows, into the Lewiston basin.

Photo Y. Aerial stereogram of the Lower Narrows outlet of the Baraboo basin of Lake Wisconsin; compare with the topographic map in Figure 13. (U.S. Department of Agriculture, Agricultural Stabilization and Conservation Service photographs WR–2JJ–15, 16, and 17, taken in 1968.)

Photo AA. The Johnstown moraine blocking the north end of the Devils Lake gorge. View to the north from South Shore Road on the south shore of Devils Lake; compare with the topographic map in Figure 19. The proglacial predecessor of Devils Lake emptied into Lake Wisconsin at first between the moraine and the west wall of the gorge and later, after the ice melted back from the moraine, through a gap in the moraine behind the building in the middle of the view.

Photo Z. The Johnstown moraine blocking the southeast end of the Devils Lake gorge. View to the west from Highway 113; compare with the topographic map in Figure 19. Sometime before the Johnstown Phase of the Wisconsin Glaciation, the Devils Lake gorge was an outlet of Lake Wisconsin, but after the Johnstown moraine blocked the gorge here, the outlet was to the northwest down the East Fork Black River.

Photo CC. The Alloa outlet of Lake Wisconsin; compare with the topographic map in Figure 39. View to the northwest from the north-bound lane of Interstate 90-94 (just south of the Highway 78 exit), across the bottom of the channel (between the highway and buildings), to the west bank of the channel against the east end of the Baraboo Hills (forested). The east bank of the channel was the glacier.

◄————————————————————————————————

Photo BB. Aerial stereogram of the Devils Lake gorge; compare with the topographic map in Figure 19. Much of the area shown here is in Devils Lake State Park. Most of the forested area is underlain by quartzite of the Baraboo Formation (Precambrian) of the South Range of the Baraboo Hills; beds of quartzite can be seen dipping to the north on the east and west sides of Devils Lake. The white areas on the walls of the gorge are talus consisting of quartzite boulders a few meters in diameter. The gorge was formed in Precambrian or Cambrian time and then filled with sediment in early Paleozoic time; the gorge was at least in part exhumed by water flowing from Lake Wisconsin. (U.S. Department of Agriculture, Agricultural Stabilization and Conservation Service photographs WR–2JJ–105, 106, 107, taken in 1968.)

Photo DD. Coarse gravel forming the foreset beds of the Alloa delta, deposited when Lake Wisconsin catastrophically drained, in the gravel pit between Shanks Road and Old U Road (southwest part of topographic map in Fig. 39). Most of the boulders are Baraboo quartzite washed from the east end of the Baraboo Hills.

Photo EE. A Sauk City terrace (foreground) cut during the catastrophic drainage of Lake Wisconsin. In the background is the Badger terrace (Johnstown outwash plain). View to the north from Trap Club Road, just east of Highway 12, 2 km west of the village of Prairie du Sac (Sec.2,T.9N.,R.6E.).

Photo FF. Wisconsin River bluffs, cut by the catastrophic flood when Lake Wisconsin drained. View down the Wisconsin River valley to the southwest, across the Sauk City terrace, northeast of the village of Arena (SE¼Sec.34,T.9N.,R.5E.). The exposed part of the bluff is the Tunnel City Formation (Cambrian).

REFERENCES

Alden, W. C., 1918, The Quaternary geology of southeastern Wisconsin with a chapter on the older rock formations: U.S. Geological Survey Professional Paper 106, 365 p.

Attig, J. W., and Clayton, L., 1986, History of late Wisconsin Permafrost in northern Wisconsin: American Quaternary Association Program with Abstracts, p. 115.

Attig, J. W., and Muldoon, M. A., 1989, Pleistocene geology of Marathon County: Wisconsin Geological and Natural History Survey Information Circular (in press).

Attig, J. W., Clayton, L., and Mickelson, D. M., 1985, Correlation of late Wisconsin glacial phases in the western Great Lakes area: Geological Society of America Bulletin, v. 96, p. 1585–1593.

Attig, J. W., Clayton, L., Bradbury, K. R., and Blanchard, M. C., 1987, Confirmation of tundra polygons and shore-ice collapse trenches in central Wisconsin and other applications of ground-penetrating radar: Geological Society of America Abstracts with Programs, v. 19, p. 187.

Attig, J. W., Clayton, L., and Mickelson, D. M., 1989a, Pleistocene stratigraphic units of Wisconsin, 1984–87: Wisconsin Geological and Natural History Survey Information Circular 62 (in press).

Attig, J. W., Mickelson, D. M., and Clayton, L., 1989b, Landform distribution and late Wisconsin glacier-bed conditions in Wisconsin: Sedimentary Geology, v. 62 (in press).

Attig, J. W., Clayton, L., Lange, K. I., and Maher, L. J., 1989c, The Ice Age geology of Devils Lake State Park: Wisconsin Geological and Natural History Survey (in press).

Baker, R. W., 1984, Pleistocene history of west-central Wisconsin: Wisconsin Geological and Natural History Survey Field Trip Guide Book 11, 76 p.

Baker, V. R., and Bunker, R. C., 1985, Cataclysmic late Pleistocene flooding from glacial Lake Missoula; A review: Quaternary Science Reviews, v. 4, p. 1–41.

Baker, V. R., and Nummedal, D., 1978, The Channeled Scablands: Washington, National Aeronautics and Space Administration, 186 p.

Bender, M. M., Bryson, R. A., and Baerreis, D. A., 1965, University of Wisconsin radiocarbon dates; 1, Radiocarbon, v. 7, p. 399–407.

——, 1971, University of Wisconsin radiocarbon dates; 9, Radiocarbon, v. 13, p. 475–486.

Black, R. F., 1974, Geology of Ice Age National Scientific Reserve of Wisconsin: National Park Service Scientific Monograph 2, 234 p.

Bretz, J H., 1950, Glacial Lake Merrimac: Illinois Academy of Science Transactions, v. 43, p. 132–136.

Brownell, J. R., 1986, Stratigraphy of unlithified deposits in the central sand plain of Wisconsin [M.S. thesis]: Madison, University of Wisconsin, 172 p.

Chamberlin, T. C., 1883, General geology, *in* Geology of Wisconsin, v. 1: Madison, Wisconsin, Commissioners of Public Printing, p. 3–300.

Clayton, L., 1984, Pleistocene geology of the Superior region, Wisconsin: Wisconsin Geological and Natural History Survey Information Circular 46, 40 p.

——, 1986, Pleistocene geology of Portage County, Wisconsin: Wisconsin Geological and Natural History Survey Information Circular 56, 19 p.

——, 1987, Pleistocene geology of Adams County, Wisconsin: Wisconsin Geological and Natural History Survey Information Circular 59, 14 p.

——, 1989a, Pleistocene geology of Wood County, Wisconsin: Wisconsin Geological and Natural History Survey Information Circular (in press).

——, 1989b, Pleistocene geology of Juneau County, Wisconsin: Wisconsin Geological and Natural History Survey Information Circular (in press).

Clayton, L., and Attig, J. W., 1987a, Lake-ice collapse trenches in Wisconsin, U.S.A.: Earth Surface Processes and Landforms, v. 12, p. 167–172.

——, 1987b, Drainage of Lake Wisconsin near the end of the Wisconsin Glaciation, *in* Mayer, L., and Nash, D., eds., Catastrophic flooding: Boston, Massachusetts, Allen and Unwin, p. 139–153.

Clayton, L., and Madison, F., 1983, Pleistocene history of the Black River Falls area: Wisconsin Geological and Natural History Survey Field Trip Guide Book 9, p. 10–13.

Clayton, L., and Moran, S. R., 1982, Chronology of late Wisconsinan glaciation in middle North America: Quaternary Science Reviews, v. 1, p. 55–82.

Dalziel, I.W.D., and Dott, R. H., Jr., 1970, Geology of the Baraboo district, Wisconsin: Wisconsin Geological and Natural History Survey Information Circular 14, 143 p.

Emery, P. A., and Seitz, H. R., 1987, Hubbard Glacier is still on the move: Geotimes, v. 32, no. 5, p. 8–9.

Eschman, D. F., and Mickelson, D. M., 1986, Correlation of glacial deposits of the Huron, Lake Michigan, and Green Bay lobes in Michigan and Wisconsin: Quaternary Science Reviews, v. 5, p. 53–57.

Flock, M. A., 1983, The late Wisconsinan Savanna Terrace in tributaries to the upper Mississippi River: Quaternary Research, v. 20, p. 165–176.

Goldthwait, J. W., 1907, Abandoned shore-lines of eastern Wisconsin: Wisconsin Geological and Natural History Survey Bulletin 17, 134 p.

Guetter, K. P., Clark, J. A., and Clayton, L., 1987, A model of glacio-isostatic tilting of glacial Lake Wisconsin shorelines: Geological Society of America Abstracts with Programs, v. 19, p. 201.

Hadley, D. W., and Pelham, J. H., 1976, Glacial deposits of Wisconsin: Wisconsin Geological and Natural History Survey Map 10, scale 1:500,000.

Harloff, N. C., 1942, Lacustrine clays of Glacial Lake Wisconsin as determined by fire protection well records [Ph.B. thesis]: Madison, University of Wisconsin, 116 p.

Johnson, W. H., 1986, Stratigraphy and correlation of the glacial deposits of the Lake Michigan Lobe prior to 14 ka BP: Quaternary Science Reviews, v. 5, p. 17–22.

Kehew, A. E., and Lord, M. L., 1987, Glacial-lake outbursts along the mid-continent margins of the Laurentide ice-sheet, *in* Mayer, L., and Nash, D., eds., Catastrophic flooding: Boston, Massachusetts, Allen and Unwin, p. 95–120.

Knox, J. C., and Attig, J. W., 1988, Geology of the pre-Illinoian sediment in the Bridgeport terrace, lower Wisconsin River valley, Wisconsin: Journal of Geology, v. 96, p. 505–513.

Larsen, C. E., 1987, Geological history of Lake Algonquin and the upper Great Lakes: U.S. Geological Survey Bulletin 1801, 36 p.

Martin, L., 1916, The physical geography of Wisconsin: Wisconsin Geological and Natural History Survey Bulletin 36, 549 p.

Mickelson, D. M., Clayton, L., Fullerton, D. S., and Borns, H. W., Jr., 1983, The late Wisconsin glacial record of the Laurentide Ice Sheet in the United States, *in* Porter, S. C., ed., Late Quaternary environments of the United States; Volume 1, The late Pleistocene: Minneapolis, University of Minnesota Press, p. 3–37.

Salisbury, R. D., and Atwood, W. W., 1900, The geography of the region about

Devil's lake and the dalles of the Wisconsin: Wisconsin Geological and Natural History Survey Bulletin 5, 151 p.

Smith, H.T.U., 1949, Periglacial features in the Driftless Area of southern Wisconsin: Journal of Geology, v. 57, p. 196–215.

Socha, B. J., 1984, The glacial geology of the Baraboo area, Wisconsin, and application of remote sensing to mapping surficial geology [M.S. thesis]: Madison, University of Wisconsin, 154 p.

Stewart, M. T., 1976, An integrated geologic, hydrologic, and geophysical investigation of drift aquifers, western Outagamie County, Wisconsin [Ph.D. thesis]: Madison, University of Wisconsin, 165 p.

Teller, J. T., and Thorliefson, L. H., 1983, The Lake Agassiz–Lake Superior connection, *in* Teller, J. T., and Clayton, L., eds., Glacial Lake Agassiz: Geological Association of Canada Special Paper 26, p. 261–290.

Thwaites, F. T., and Bertrand, K., 1957, Pleistocene geology of the Door Peninsula, Wisconsin: Geological Society of America Bulletin, v. 68, p. 831–880.

Thwaites, F. T., and Twenhofel, W. H., 1921, Windrow Formation; An upland gravel formation of the Driftless and adjacent areas of the upper Mississippi valley: Geological Society of America Bulletin, v. 32, p. 293–314.

Weidman, S., 1907, The geology of north central Wisconsin: Wisconsin Geological and Natural History Survey Bulletin 16, 697 p.

Wright, H. E., Jr., 1973, Tunnel valleys, glacial surges, and subglacial hydrology of the Superior Lobe, Minnesota: Geological Society of America Memoir 136, p. 251–276.

MANUSCRIPT ACCEPTED BY THE SOCIETY MARCH 10, 1989

Typeset by WESType Publishing Services, Inc., Boulder, Colorado
Printed in U.S.A. by Malloy Lithographing, Inc., Ann Arbor, Michigan